WINNING
IN THE
BATTLES OF
LIFE

CHRISTINE FRANCIS

authorHOUSE®

AuthorHouse™ LLC
1663 Liberty Drive
Bloomington, IN 47403
www.authorhouse.com
Phone: 1-800-839-8640

Scripture quotations marked KJV are from the Holy Bible, King James Version (Authorized Version). First published in 1611. Quoted from the KJV Classic Reference Bible, Copyright © 1983 by The Zondervan Corporation.

Published by AuthorHouse   08/14/2014

ISBN: 978-1-4918-6610-8 (sc)
ISBN: 978-1-4918-6609-2 (hc)
ISBN: 978-1-4918-6608-5 (e)

Library of Congress Control Number: 2014903261

CONTENTS

Dedication vii

Foreword... ix

Acknowledgements.. xi

Introduction.. xiii

Preface xvii

Chapter 1:   Dominion, The Starting Point 1

Chapter 2:   Be Confident and Courageous............................ 9

Chapter 3:   The Jericho Battle 15

Chapter 4:   The Holy Spirit In Battle 28

Chapter 5:   Winning In the Face Adversity 43

Chapter 6:   Praises, the Joy of Winning............................... 50

Chapter 7:   Humilty, the Main Ingredient 58

Chapter 8:   Conquering Self, The Worst Enemy................... 65

Chapter 9:   Kneeling Determines Winning.......................... 71

Chapter 10: The Turn Around Experience............................. 84

DEDICATION

The Holy Spirit, whose power helps us win in all battles of life.

FOREWORD

This book is a wakeup call to believers and everyone who has lost hope in the face of life's challenges. God is still in the business of fighting and winning for His children.

Kera Segun-Oludipe

ACKNOWLEDGEMENTS

All glory, praise and honor to God Almighty who made this work a reality.

I praise God for the life of my father in the faith, Bishop David Oyedepo, through whom I have been more enlightened in the Word of God.

My thanks go to my family for their support throughout the period of putting this work together especially my latest grandson, Olaoluwa Chukwuebuka Oludipe, for his patience during the editing of this book by his mother.

A big thank you to my daughter, Kera Segun-Oludipe, for proof reading and editing this book. God bless you.

I love you all!

INTRODUCTION

Winning implies the idea of someone being in a competition (or a race) in which one desires to come out successful. When this happens, such person is declared a "winner". A winner, therefore, describes someone who wins in all areas of life—(both in) spiritual and physical (race [life]). The prize or reward to such individuals is attested to by Apostle Paul in the book of Corinthians: (There is a prize or reward given to such individuals. In the Christian race the Scripture had this to say,)

> *"Know ye not that they which run in a race run all, but one receiveth the price? So run, that ye may obtain".*
>
> *[1 Cor. 9:24]*

Furthermore, Apostle Paul wrote about the incorruptible crown [vs. 25] which is the reward for all who win the heavenly race. This refers to the victory of gaining eternal salvation, i.e. the precious goal of the Christian life. This goal can only be achieved by giving up some of our rights for the sake of others and by renouncing sin, Satan (and the world,) and those things that would distract us from the race altogether.

There are many kinds of winning. In this book, however, we shall be dealing with the Christian race. How we can run, win and obtain the promises of God. We shall also be discussing what could be barriers, pitfalls, disturbances and problems in this life, for which, by the grace of God, we shall also learn from the examples of other people's experience, how to escape such miserable situations.

We shall be discussing certain positive attitudes that can help us reach our goal and of course, obtain the attendant rewards. The Bible teaches and encourages that we believes, by faith, the Savior and Lord Jesus Christ who died on the cross of Calvary to redeem mankind. By Him also comes winning as it were, for no one can escape life's hurdles without the Master who knows the way.

> *"But what saith it? The word is nigh thee, even in thy mouth, and in thy heart: that is, the word of faith, which we preach; That if thou shalt confess with thy mouth the Lord Jesus, and shalt believe in thine heart that God hath raised him from the dead, thou shalt be saved. For with the heart man believeth unto righteousness; and with the mouth confession is made unto salvation".*
> *[Rom. 10: 8-10]—KJV*

The essentials of salvation are summarized in the above referenced passage. Our Lord Jesus and His bodily resurrection is the center of the Christian belief. Faith, when established in one's heart, is evidenced in the emotions, intellect, the will and totality of the believers' persona. In the same vein, confession must be made that Jesus is the Savior and the Lord of one's life. When this is done the heavenly race has begun. "Savior" connotes He died in your place to set you free and "Lord" means having power, dominion, authority and the right to be your Master.

Until all these are done, no one wins the battle of life that ends in eternity with Christ. The back-up you need to fight with and win is only found in Jesus' sacrifice on the cross. His blood fights and wins for you all through your life-time and the life to come if only you key in. It is very necessary because what lies ahead in life is tough. You can't fight all by yourself and defeat Satan, the devil. Jesus had already won the battle but you need to believe, accept He did, before it can work for you. The earlier you do this, the better for you. You are a winner as you accept, today, the Lord Jesus into your life, and you will continue to WIN in Jesus precious name, Amen.

"Battle" implies tough and difficult situation, very hard to deal with. It is to compete with someone with the aim of achieving the opposite of what they are trying to achieve.

The Israelites were faced with a tough battle against the Philistines and giant Goliath. The Anointing in David's life took over the battle and all through his life it was this anointing that made him a conqueror. Anointing makes the difference in the lives of those who identify with God (pay the price). How in the world could a lad kill the giant if not for God's anointing upon his life? You can believe, as I do, that God fights the battle of all those who trust in Him.

> *"And all this assembly shall know that the LORD saveth not with sword and spear: for the battle is the LORD's, and he will give you into our hands".*
>
> *[1 Samuel 17:47]*

My joy is that the battle we are faced with had been won by our Savior Jesus Christ, the Anointed one. The referenced scripture above explains the fight of faith David engaged in against Goliath. A study of that chapter helps us see God as fighting our battles of life, hence faith in Him is involved. David's victory over Goliath is as a result of his unfeigned faith in God that had been tested and proven in his life when he killed the bear and tore the lion as they came to ravage his father's sheep. Today, all problems facing you, as Goliath, are destroyed in Jesus name. Amen!

What Were The Ingredients in David's Heart?

a. David had a heart for God. He loved and looked up to God all the time. [1Chro. 16:11, 1Samuel 16:11-13]. He was anointed for a purpose.

b. David had deep concern for the honor and reputation of the Lord God of Israel. [1Sam 17:26, 36 & 46].

c. David's confidence in the Lord's might have been strengthened by his memory of the previous times when he had prayed for and experienced God's deliverance. [1Sam 17:34-37].

    d.   David did not boast or trust in himself but in God, to achieve the victory over Goliath and the Philistines [1 Samuel 17:37, 45-47].

    e.   The Spirit of the Lord was mightily upon David. It is never by our power or our might but by God's Spirit [Zech. 4:6].

Our lives solely depend on God, and would have meaning and victories when we allow Him take charge. Like David, we can trust and have faith in God when we face oppositions or seemingly insurmountable problems and situations. Giants or challenges in life can be overcome if we exercise faith like David and depend upon the power of the Holy Spirit. Jesus, our immortal Redeemer, had paid pricelessly for our lives and gave us dominion.

Whatever situation we find ourselves in, let us emulate David in the exercise of our faith. Remember, the attitude we adopt determines our respective victories. We can either perceive it as mountain or bread to eat; it all depends on our beliefs and the attitude we bring to bear. Confession brings possessions. Rejoice always, hoping to win.

PREFACE

"Behold, I give unto you power to tread upon serpents and scorpions, and over all the power of the enemy: and nothing shall by any means hurt you".

[Luke 10: 19]

Who are serpents and scorpions? These are the problems of life! The Bible refers to them as reptiles you can crush under feet (or anyway you choose to deal with them). The important fact is they are what you can kill fast. Power of the enemy refers to sicknesses, ups and downs of life, troubles and circumstances of all sorts. Choosing how to handle them is your responsibility, either positively or negatively.

There was this man in the Bible who was confined to his sick bed for thirty eight years. His family and friends deserted him and the battle against loneliness and deadly disease wrapped him in. He spent thirty eight years waiting to be helped into the pool, once stirred, to be healed. He never tried to do something, just wallowing in self pity and negative attitude. I can only imagine him grumbling and murmuring against people he felt could come to his rescue. One day he got help but was still muttering excuses. He said, "I want to be healed but cannot get anyone to throw me into the pool when the angel moves the water". He continued, as I want to, another goes before me! Still there ready to take more years. But when our Lord Jesus commanded him to get up, take his mat and go home, he received his healing instantly. [John 5:1-8]

Do you see it was his choice to lie there for years, had he wiggled a little, get stirred up in heart and take steps of faith, he would have made it.

This shows that David's type of spirit is "take it by force" kind of which is the positive attitude.

'Arise and shine' is the command in Isaiah. 60:1; you are to pursue greatness in life, pursue good enjoyable life in the perspective of looking unto God not man. Brother Paul admonished us to put on all the armor of God to crush satanic forces geared towards our lives.

God through Jesus had called us to become inheritors of the Kingdom; we should not be afraid of challenges of life but put on the Lord Jesus. Our lives had been secured in that Blood He shed for us on the cross at Calvary. He gave the assurance, promises and power that can beat the enemy down before our faces as we engage the fight of faith and winning is ours, praise the Lord! His wisdom brings us to the state of being always in the atmosphere of authority. Winning is mine. Amen and Amen!

The Christian race is a spiritual one, it is not by our power or what we can accomplish on our own, but our Energizer, the Holy Spirit, supplies the power, wisdom and strength. He is the Illuminator, Comforter, Teacher, and the only source of winning. The Holy Spirit wins for all who had given Jesus Christ the opportunity to rule their lives. These are the washed in the blood, who have accepted His offer of Salvation, made Him Personal Lord and Savior of their lives.

> *". . . . if thou shall confess with thy mouth the Lord Jesus, and shall believe in thine heart that God hath raised Him from the dead, thou shall be saved. For with the heart man believeth unto righteousness; and with the mouth confession is made unto salvation".*
>
> *[Romans 10:9-10]*

Jesus has conquered death, sorrow and everything that will want to rise up against our lives. We shall be exploring whom the Holy Spirit is, how He guides, teaches, so we learn how to be winners at all times. It's Jesus, Jesus, and Jesus only!!!

Am excited about the life we have been called to live. Read this with me

". . . . Eye has not seen, nor ear heard, neither have entered into the heart of man, the things which God hath prepared for them that love Him"

[1 Cor. 2: 9]

The Christian life is a great life. God would not let anyone see what He had prepared for all those who will obey Him. From the beginning Adam the first man disobeyed God and was chased out of Eden. Jesus Christ, the second Adam, came, obeyed God, died on the Cross; brought a new life to mankind. Now all people who will make Jesus Christ the Lord of their lives will inherit these things God had hidden from ages. Is that not interesting, would you not desire to be one in the number?

On the cross our Lord Jesus suffered and gave you everlasting life. That is, He dealt with death [second death], which is everlasting separation from God and all He had prepared. Be informed that you lost sorrow, pain, sickness, demonic attacks, poverty, anger, hatred, desperations and all the enemies of man, when Jesus died on the Cross. You were furnished with a new life, dominion, power from on high that helps you to win battles of life without stress, Hallelujah!!! God is love; His loving kindness is from one generation to another. It is an enjoyable, glorious encounter which will turn your life around for good forever. It is a change of life you will be glad about. God has offered you an everlasting celebration of life as you join this wagon of full life and glorious living in faith by Christ Jesus.

You are wonderfully and fearfully made and cannot afford to loose sight of the heavenly bliss with this wonderful Savior who gave His life for you. The great and higher life He brought to the world is yours too. High life in Christ Jesus opens you to victories over all circumstances that would crop up as difficulties in your life. God had made you a success through the death of Jesus on the Cross; you can become a stumbling block to your destiny by refusing the offer of Salvation which is the starting point where all the successes begin.

Dominion in Christ brings all it takes to be a winner in all battles in life. Battles are real in life, but victory is more real to believers in Christ. You do not win by whom you know or how wealthy you are, but by the Holy Ghost. Christ, the Anointed One, supplies the power and the strength you need [Psalms 18:39]. God who gave David and others the power to win will surely do same for you. You are about to feed with words that will open the heavens and shower you with blessings. Have a pleasurable reading!!!

ONE

DOMINION, THE STARTING POINT

In the beginning when God created all things, man also was created by God and dominion was given to him. When you closely check the account of creation in the Bible, you will see that God consciously made man after His Image. Both men and women were special creations of God, not a product of evolution. They were both created in the image and likeness of God. On this basic fact, they could respond to and have fellowship with God and uniquely reflect God's love, glory, and holiness. They were to do this by knowing and obeying God. Let's read the Bible account in Genesis.

"And God said; let us make man in our image, after our likeness: and let them have dominion over the fish of the sea, and over the fowl of the air, and over the cattle, and over all the earth, and over every creeping thing that creepeth upon the earth. So God created man in His own image, in the image of God created He him; male and female created He them"

Gen.1:26-27

Although they were sinless and holy possessing wisdom, a heart of love and will to do right, Adam and Eve had personal fellowship with God that involved moral obedience and intimate relationship or communion. Their dominion was overthrown and they were chased out of Eden, they also lost their dominion, fellowship and communion with God and curses were laid upon man.

> *"And the LORD God said unto the serpent, Because thou hast done this, thou [art] cursed above all cattle, and above every beast of the field; upon thy belly shalt thou go, and dust shalt thou eat all the days of thy life: and I will put enmity between thee and the woman, and between thy seed and her seed; it shall bruise thy head, and thou shalt bruise his heel. Unto the woman he said, I will greatly multiply thy sorrow and thy conception; in sorrow thou shalt bring forth children; and thy desire [shall be] to thy husband, and he shall rule over thee. And unto Adam he said, Because thou hast hearkened unto the voice of thy wife, and hast eaten of the tree, of which I commanded thee, saying, Thou shalt not eat of it: cursed [is] the ground for thy sake; in sorrow shalt thou eat [of] it all the days of thy life; Thorns also and thistles shall it bring forth to thee; and thou shalt eat the herb of the field; In the sweat of thy face shalt thou eat bread, till thou return unto the ground; for out of it wast thou taken: for dust thou [art], and unto dust shalt thou return."*
>
> *[Gen. 3:14-19]*

What was the reason for their fall? Adam and Eve attempted to set themselves up as God's equals and to determine their own standards. Through their fall, human beings became to some extent independent of God and chose for themselves good or evil. Satan gained power over them and the entire human race. They sold themselves and the whole earth to Satan, as a result of the fall the whole world was rolled into depravity, and man lost the dominion.

The world and the human race were doomed to Satan's rule. Satan became the god of this world and blinded the eyes of people to the truth of the Gospel.

> *"But if our Gospel be hid, it is hid to them that are lost:*
>
> *In whom the god of this world hath blinded the minds of them which believe not, lest the light of the glorious gospel of Christ, who is the image of God shine unto them"*
>
> *[11Cor. 4:3-4]*

However God so loved the human race that He determined to conquer Satan, reconcile man and the world to Himself at the cost of His Son's life [Jn. 3:16].

God in His Infinite mercy did not leave man in shame. He thought of good plans to rescue man immediately, to bring man out of shame of nakedness, disgrace and sin [Gen. 3:21]; God made atonement for man by the blood of the animal and also used the skin to cover man. God promised He will bruise Satan's head, which He did when Jesus brought us salvation. All through the Old Testament the blood of animals were being used for temporal atonement. Jesus Christ the Mediator of the new covenant died once and for all and completely redeemed man from the bondage of Satan. His blood is forever perfected for the cleansing of all who trust in Him.

> *"But Christ being come an high Priest of good things to come, by a greater and more perfect tabernacle not made with hands, that is to say, not of this building; Neither by the blood of goats and calves, but by His own blood He entered in once into the holy place, having obtained eternal redemption for us. For if the blood of bulls and of goats, and the ashes of an heifer sprinkling the unclean, sanctified to the purifying of the flesh: How much more shall the blood of Christ who through the eternal Spirit offered Himself without spot to God, purge your conscience from dead works to serve the Living God"*
>
> *[Hebrew 9:11-14]*

Acceptance of the penalty, (the death of Christ on the cross of Calvary), by faith is and remains the only way for man to escape destruction, hell and eternal separation from God which is the greatest battle in life. During His death on the cross, Christ gave up Himself freely; shed His innocent blood in order to delete your sins and to reconcile you back to God. Therefore if you accept the offer, you have made peace with God. Most times you see man seeking to be at peace with God when he has not made peace with God. First thing should be, make peace with God through His Son Jesus and then seek to be at peace with Him. [Romans 5:1].

3

The blood of Christ accomplished the following;

a. His blood forgives the sins of all who believe and repent [Mathew 26:28, Eph.1:7].

b. His blood ransoms all believers from the wicked plans and power of Satan [1Peter 1:18-19, Rev.5:9].

c. His blood justifies all who believe in Him [Romans 3:24-25].

d. His blood cleanses the believers' conscience that he might serve God without guilt in full assurance [Hebrew 9:14, 10:22].

e. His blood opens the way for believers to come directly before God in order to find grace, mercy, help and salvation [Hebrew 7:25, 10:19, Matt.26:28].

f. The saving, reconciling power and the purifying agent in the blood of Jesus is continually appropriated to the believer as he draws near to God through Christ [1John 1:7, Hebrew 7:25].

Jesus' Blood is effective forever to all people [including you] who trust in Him. In the Old Testament, Israelis were shielded by the blood of the Passover lamb which they strike on their door posts [Exodus 12:1-30]. God's deliverance of the Israelis from slavery in Egypt is one event that cannot be overemphasized because of the blood covenant. Today Jesus' blood is still available for anyone who wants to be free from the bondage of Satan and the world. As the angel of death passed over the homes of the Israelis because of the blood of the lamb, the same way second death, sorrow, pain, sickness, poverty, etc pass over the homes of all those who trust in the Blood of Christ our Savior. We are free from the doom of the evil one [Revelation 20: 11-15].

The blood covenant provided covering and protection for the people of God as they crossed the Red sea. Atonement with the blood of bull and goat however was never going to be enough because the sacrifice is yearly i.e. shedding of the animal blood [Hebrew 8]. The high priest also needed to go in once a year but not without blood. It was a practice of risk for the high priest who goes in there because he may loose his life at a trace of mistake or sin in his life. For this, God thought it wise to come to our rescue with a better covenant; the blood of Jesus which is perfected forever. Beloved, your dominion is restored only through faith in the blood of Jesus Christ.

> *". . . . as many as received Him to them gave He power [DOMINION] to become the sons of God . . . ."*
>
> *[John 1:12]*

Power to become strong and adequately prepared has been given to whosoever wants to fight life's battle. Everyone fights some kind of battle and it is important you know the enemy and use the provision of God which is found only in the blood of Christ. It is also good you understand that this enemy is not your co-worker, your mom or dad, your brother or any of your relation. Satan is the enemy of man since the beginning of the world and fights without rest to win you to his doom.

We had been admonished to love our enemies [flesh and blood enemies] not devil and his co-horts because they are master minds of all kinds of contention and troubles. So knowing this, we reach out to the only power that can help us fight; the power in the blood of Jesus Christ.

How Powerful Is The Blood Of Jesus?

Blood is the fluid in human beings. The Bible uses it primarily as a symbol of life and death. Without the blood there is no life. Leviticus 17:11 says, every life of the flesh is in the blood. Hebrew 9:22 also says, without shedding of blood is no remission of sin. This clearly spells out that the blood sacrifice of animals in the Old Testament represents death as punishment for sin. This establishes the point that without the shedding of the blood there is no forgiveness of sins.

Animal blood sacrifices in the Old Testament fore-shadows the blood of Christ and His death on the cross as penalty for our sins. Through this blood presented to God in heaven, we obtain forgiveness, release from bondage, atonement, justification, victory, holiness etc. The power in His blood saves, redeems, and sets at liberty all who by faith believes in Him. Substitution by the blood of another [the animals] helps us understand the importance of the blood of Christ so we receive our salvation under the new covenant. When Jesus Christ spilled His blood on the cross, He substituted His life for the sinner's life [Rom. 5:1].

Since Jesus' life is without sin and is perfect before God, we are all called to perfect salvation for in Him only we have redemption [Colossians 1:14, Hebrew 9:13-14, Revelation 7:14].

We are sanctified by this one offering and it is efficacious forever. Perfect salvation in Christ is imparted by grace to all people; regardless of tribe or tongue so long they come by faith. They are imparted by the Holy Spirit of God to live for Jesus Christ. Faith in this context can be defined as sincerely coming to God and believing in His goodness [Heb. 11:6]. So drawing near and faith is inseparable in this case. By drawing near to God through Christ one finds mercy, grace help, salvation sanctification and holiness. All these imply that where there is no drawing near to God in prayer and fellowship with Christ, there is no saving faith.

Blood is thicker than water we say; Abel's blood cried to God for vengeance when his brother, Cain killed him [Genesis 4:1-12], but the blood of Jesus cried out for the whole Universe. From Calvary to mountains and also to the deepest valley: for the cleansing of man and to save man from sin and bondage. His blood declared justice had been done, the curse upon earth had been lifted, mankind is restored and forgiven, and dominion took its rightful place. Let's celebrate Jesus wow!!! He had restored us back to dominion, Hallelujah-Amen!!!

I like to see things as they are, so let's read the scripture below,

> *"In whom we have redemption through His blood, the forgiveness of sin, according to the riches of His glory"*
> *[Ephesians 1:7]*

> *"And they overcame him by the blood of the Lamb . . . ."*
> *[Revelation 12:11]*

"And having made peace through the blood of His cross, by Him to reconcile all unto Himself . . ."

[Col. 1:20]

Can you please take a good look at those scriptures and see what great things the blood of Jesus does. Jesus was not out for any game show. He is optimistic of what His vision is. He could have told His Father, I can't bear it anymore, let go of this mess, and the world can go to hell I do not care. But no, He had compassion and died for us. What a loving Savoir, what a glorious mission to save the whole world. He was not self centered, not mindful of His riches, power and glories. But obediently came, although He knew what He would face, the sufferings, shame, reproach, insults and beatings, dying on the cross, yet He did not decline from the assignment. He gave Himself totally to be offered as the Lamb of God. Thank God for God who thought of you and I, out of mercy, He reached out to save us. God is love and would not leave us in doom forever.

We are His Image, we are to respond to this love and willingly give our lives to Him. God is calling you now, can you hear Him? Do not give deaf ears to His voice. Do not harden your heart. Jesus' inheritance and all that God promised is waiting for you. Christ's death took away your shame, fear, retrogression, oppositions, disappointments, etc and brought you love, salvation, prosperity, good health, enlistment to the kingdom of God. He gave you power to live in righteousness, holiness, open doors, wealth. The earth-quake shook and swallowed all your enemies as Christ gave up the ghost on the cross and put Satan under your feet. You were restored and renewed Hallelujah!!! When He said "it is finished" all battles of your life were settled, they were made bread for you to eat. When He arose, you rose from all odds to your blessed destiny . . . Praise God! It is time to live life eternal in Christ!

How can you escape the terrible judgment if you refuse to fully respond to God's call today? Brethren, we have been made a kingdom of priests. We are God's own treasured possessions. Even though all nations are accountable to God because He created them, believers in Christ in all nations have unique relationship with God because He is our Redeemer. God's purpose for Israel foreshadowed his purpose for the Church

[Body of Christ]. So we have to pledge our allegiance to the Almighty God who is the beginning and end of our lives.

Give ear to His Word of eternal life; you are a winner in all battles of this life and that to come. We ought to be thankful ever to God that has saved us. There is only one name Jesus Christ, in Him only salvation is found [Acts 4:12]. He is the Lord of lords, the King of kings, the Ancient of days, the Fountain of life, the Everlasting God, the Immortal Redeemer, the Mighty Savior, the Lord of all, Hallelujah!!! Let all glory be to Him forever, Amen.

—— TWO ——

BE CONFIDENT AND COURAGEOUS

"Be strong and of good courage: for unto this people thou shall divide for an inheritance the land, which I swore unto their fathers to give them. Only be thou strong and very courageous, that thou mayest observe to do according to all the law . . . ."

[Joshua 1:6-7]

Courage is the quality of mind or spirit that enables a person to face difficulty, danger, pain, etc without fear; bravery. Being courageous has to do with ability to brace up to challenges anytime and anywhere. It is a mindset that helps you conquer challenges as they come in their sizes, shapes and designs. Moses, in the wilderness, was backed up or guided by the Spirit of God. The men and women of today are also guided by the Holy Spirit to persevere or suffer long in courage as they work in God's Vineyard. If you can yield to God's spirit you will also be courageous and finish strong. God told Joshua that with a courageous mindset no one will be able to stand before him.

"There shall not any man be able to stand before thee all the days of thy life: as I was with Moses, so I will be with thee: I will not fail thee, nor forsake thee.

Be strong and of a good courage: for unto this people shall thou divide for an inheritance the land which I sware unto their fathers to give them.

> *Only be thou strong and very courageous, that thou mayest observe to do according to all the law, which Moses my servant commanded thee: turn not from it to the right hand or to the left, that thou mayest prosper wither so ever thou goest.*
>
> ***Joshua 1:5-7***

God's word is sure and authentic. When He says 'I will be with you, I will not fail you, nor forsake you'; He means it. So where ever you go, all that you put your hands to do, He is there with you! What an undeniable promise. The fact that He will not leave you to walk alone is enough courage for you. Observing to do all He has commanded results in winning of battles. The problem with many children of God is emulation; imitate people. If you stick to God's instructions definitely your victory is guaranteed. The moment our ears are open and hearts yielding to His Spirit, there is nothing we cannot do. God is not a liar, when He says it, He does it. God knows the end from the beginning, there is none else beside Him . . . [Isaiah 46:9-11].

Tough People Do Not Quit

Beloved of God, various problems and troubles of life you are facing now are pebbles before you, no longer mountains. This is true for a believer in Christ. You may say "my own is different" so tough and scary or mighty to tackle. Be reminded that God is greater or mightier than all these problems before you. There is no mountain He cannot climb or big ocean that He cannot swim [Isaiah 43:2]. David was faced with Goliath, Esther was faced with annihilation with her people, Hannah was faced with barrenness, etc. God saw all of those through, in the same vein, see yourself coming out victoriously from that challenge you are facing now. In the book of Isaiah 40:28-31[read], you will see clearly that God gives strength to go through tough times.

In my own life, I have faced too many difficult times, almost on the brink of trauma that could lead to losing my life, I mean death became apparent. But in all I trusted God and stood by an unshakable faith. All through the horror or frightful dark hours I said to myself, God you are my anchor. I turned to the studying of God's word, not allowing myself to be carried away by the circumstances I was faced with. [11Cor.

5:7]. Through it all I was victorious. Tough people do not quit! It is said that winners don't quit and quitters don't win. Holding unto God courageously results in double victory.

Joshua courageously led the Israelites to the promise land after Moses died. This was a national task and must be fulfilled. Nehemiah and Elijah were faced with national challenges too! The former was told how Jerusalem and her gates were burnt down with fire; the remnant in great affliction and reproach in a province and in captivity too. What did Nehemiah do? He broke down in tears, but did not stop there. Courageously he got up and prayed to God; he confessed the sins of his people, repented in dust and ashes and asked God's mercies and forgiveness. God granted his requests and favored him [Neh.1:1-11, 2:1-8]. Elijah, on the other hand, challenged the prophets of Baal and dangerously stood against the idol worshippers [1Kgs 18:21-40]. He was so courageous that he faced them all by himself and God stood by him.

Fainting or being afraid in the face of adversity is only natural however I charge you to look unto JESUS (Hebrews 12:2). The moment the enemy sees you are afraid; he comes on with a force to swallow you up. Your strong willed heart of faith in the word of God makes him panic. God's illumination in your life scares him. That is why you must get hold of the right fellowship with your Savior Jesus. Hold unto His promises, for they never fail.

Let us take a look at these scriptures for insight;

> *"Be strong and of good courage, fear not, nor be afraid of them: for the Lord thy God: he it is that doth go with thee; he will not fail thee, nor forsake thee"*
>
> ### *Deut. 31:6, cf, Heb. 13:5b*

> *"And Joshua said unto them, fear not, nor be dismayed. Be strong and of good courage: for thus shall the Lord do to all your enemies against whom ye fight"*
>
> ### *[Josh. 10:2]*

"Be of good courage, and let us behave ourselves valiantly for our people and for the cities of our God; and let the Lord do that which is good in his sight"

1Chro.19:13

"And David said to Solomon his son, be strong and of good courage, and do it, fear not nor be dismayed: for the Lord even my God will be with thee; he will not fail thee; nor forsake thee, until thou has finished all the work for the service of the house of the Lord"

1Chro.28:20

"Though an host shall encamp against me, my heart shall not fear: though war should rise against, in this will I be confident"

Psalms 27:3

"Therefore will we not fear, though the earth be removed, and though the mountains be carried into the midst of the sea; though the waters thereof roar and be troubled, though the mountain shake with the swellings thereof . . ."

Psalms 46:2-3

All created life is frail and weak and will ultimately come to an end, but God's word endures forever. God's promises will be fulfilled; His redemptive truth cannot be annulled or changed. The Israelis would have been swallowed up by Pharaoh the adversary. All through their battle in slavery, God was with them. They faced battle in all areas of their lives; mentally, physically, economically, socially, academically, materially, but with courage in the word of God through Moses they left Egypt and crossed through the middle of the Red Sea unhurt. Remember the water parted and they went through and if it returns to its position, they would be at risk of drowning, but they believed Moses' word from God. This was an act of faith.

We have been admonished to meditate on the word, and then we shall succeed [Josh 1:8]. Make up your mind to believe and stand upon it, your faith walk must be strong. You need to dwell in the secret place of the Most high for defense; find time to search God's word and pitch your tent on it unmovable. David knew the secret so well. His faith is such that he never gets tired. But like every human he got discouraged when his enemies burnt down the city of Ziklag where he resides. They did not only burn down the place, but took all they could find away. The women and their sons and daughters were taken captives. David's two wives and children inclusive; so he and his men wept sore until they had no power to weep.

At this time he was distressed greatly more so when his men moved to stone him to death. He rose up and encouraged himself in the Lord his God. He quickly asked God what he should do. Taking correct measures as God instructed him, he and his men recovered all[1Sam.30:1-8,18-19]. This is being courageous in the face of hopelessness. You may be at the cross road now, what do you do? Go to God and receive instructions. Go pick up your Bible and see Psalm 91, by the time you are done not only will you be encouraged but you will tear your enemies apart and recover all Hallelujah!!

He that dwell means; you come to a place in your life when you throw earthly things aside and resolve to focus on God's word for every inch of moves. You dwell therein not letting fear, doubt, worry etc, pull you down. Apply God's word to all areas of your life. It is your armory; you can't go anywhere or do anything without it.

> *"Finally, my brethren, be strong in the Lord, and in the power of His might. Put on the whole armor of God that ye may be able to stand against the wiles of the devil. For we wrestle not against flesh and blood, but against principalities, against powers, against the rulers of the darkness of this world, against spiritual wickedness in the high places. Wherefore take unto you the whole armor of God that ye may be able to withstand in the evil day, and having done all, to stand. Stand therefore, having your loins gird about with truth, and having on the breastplate of righteousness: and your feet shod with the preparation of the gospel of peace; above all, taking the shield of faith, wherewith ye shall be able to quench all the fiery darts of the wicked. And take the helmet of salvation and the sword of the Spirit, which is the Word of God . . . ."*
> *[Ephesians 6:10-17]*

The above Scripture connotes war. All believers in Christ are engaged in a serious spiritual conflict with the evil forces. It is warfare of faith and continues till we enter the life to come. The good news here is that your victory had been secured by Christ Himself through His death on the Cross. Jesus waged a triumphant battle against Satan, disarmed the evil powers, authorities of wickedness. Let's read,

> *"Blotting out the handwriting of ordinances that was against us, which was contrary to us, and took it out of the way, nailing it to the cross;*
>
> *And having spoiled principalities and powers, he made a show of them openly, triumphing over them in it"*
>
> *[Colossians 2:14-15]*

The code or agreement against us was deleted by Christ's death on the cross. Think of it this way, all sins forgiven, the slat wiped clean, that old arrest warrant cancelled and nailed to the cross. It did not stop there; He stripped all the spiritual tyrants in the universe of their sham authority at the cross and marched them naked through the streets. No more shackles, no more pain, no more chains, no more bondage. We are free!

Before Christ died you were not able to respond to God. But now Jesus had destroyed all of Satan's tricks. You lose or win in life depending on how you open your mind to the teachings of grace you have received. The moment you stick it right down in your heart that Jesus had finished all struggles over life, your winning is sure. Victory must be won in the spiritual before you overcome in the physical. Beloved, be bold and take what belongs to you.

> *"Now thanks be unto God, which always causeth us to triumph in Christ ..."*
>
> *[11Cor. 2:14]*

THREE

THE JERICHO BATTLE

Let's go back to how the Israelis won their battles. Joshua was instructed by God to lead the children of Israel and match round Jericho.

> *"Now Jericho was straitly shut up because of the children of Israel none went out, and none came in. And Lord said unto Joshua, See, I have given into thine hand Jericho, and the king thereof; and the mighty men of valor"*
>
> *[Joshua 6:1-2]*

The city covered about eight acres and was a fortressed city not just for its residents but also for the inhabitants of the nearby country sides. Jericho's fenced walls were about thirty feet high and twenty feet thick.

They were protected by the gods of Canaanites. Now Joshua and the Israelis have to go through this city. It was going to be tough but not for God of Israel. The capture of Jericho is important and would be key to Joshua's war strategy, for it would demonstrate that their God was superior to the Canaanites gods.

But how will they overcome this battle? What they did was to hearken to God's command; to go round the city six times and on the seventh, they shall blast the trumpet, and shall shout greatly, then the city walls will fall [vs.3-5]. They, after this, went into the city and destroyed all the people, animals . . . [vs.20-21]. Note that the city was brought down by God's direct act as the Israelis obeyed His voice. It is never by our strength or power. The Israelis had to fight their way into possessing the land of Jericho. Remember it is a promised land nevertheless they had to dispossess the land from them that lived there at the time. Victory becomes surety because God is involved. Has He promised and will not keep it? Joshua was confident leading the people as Moses did however God had to make them ready for the war [Josh. 5:2-7], They were to be circumcised to roll away the reproach of Egypt.

Like the Israelis, God has given us a command to be circumcised through the blood of Jesus. Without obedience to God we lose fights and all wars waged by satanic forces. Ignorance is not an excuse, you got to accept the mercy and grace God had provided through Jesus Christ before you can win these battles. Knowledge and understanding God's word puts your feet on the floor against the devil. God wants you to come as you are even though your sins are red like crimson; the promise is you will be washed anew! The old ways of life must be thrown aside, forgive your-self and make a turn to the cleansing blood of Christ. This way you are ready for a life of a victor.

Obedience to God who owns us and has all power to create or destroy brings down our wars to nothing.

Obedience to God's word results to winning wars that pose threats to our lives. What if you decide today to obey the voice of God? Then you will begin to experience how He fights the battles for they that obey Him. Or will you reject and proudly think you do not need God? See, it is for you to decide how you will live your life on earth; whether to enjoy it or suffer through it (2 Peter.1:3). Whom you follow determines your end! Satan was filled with pride and was thrown down from heaven [See, Isaiah 14:13-15, Ezekiel 28:15-18], to hell which has become his final place of torment. Satan was once the Anointed [cherub] Angel, but pride made him land in hell fire. Since then he's been fighting to seduce those who had given deaf ears to the voice of God. The only escape is to get hold of the word of God, study, meditate on it and live by it and you have Satan under your feet and his schemes, defeated. God had made you His battle axe and weapon of warfare. He says, with you He will break in pieces the nations and destroy kingdoms.

"Thou art my battle axe and weapons of war: for with thee will I break in pieces the nations, and with thee will I destroy kingdoms;

And with thee will I break in pieces the horse and the rider; and with thee will I break in pieces the chariot and his rider;

With thee also will I break in pieces man and woman; and with thee will I break in pieces old and young; and with thee will I break in pieces the young man and the maid;

I will also break in pieces with thee the shepherd and his flock; and with thee will I break in pieces the husbandman and his yoke of oxen; and with thee will I break in pieces captains and rulers."
[Jeremiah 51:20-23]

The Christian fight of faith is the only thing worth fighting for. Amidst trials, difficulties, temptations, molestations and all sorts of oppositions, our Lord Jesus Christ fought and won. His love reigns supreme in the lives of His children. In the midst of situations and circumstances His love shines on you and is real; He said nothing can separate you from this love. The triumphant victory had been won and is yours.

Remember also that love is another weapon we can fight our battles with. Compassion flows when love is in action. Jesus' love made Him to give up his life for us (John.3:16, 10:17-18). He did this to set us free from Satan's bondage.

The love David and Jonathan shared, like brothers, helped David stay alive (1Sam.18:1-3, 19:1-7)

We got to follow His example, go out of our ways to love and bring our world to God their Maker. Love in the home, in our communities, churches, schools, everywhere can be so amazingly used to fight battles of life. It is only sacrificial love, love that is not selfish or self-centered that wins the entire war the enemy holds against us in this life. The grace and love of God helps us to go through rejection, abuse, ridicule, suffering and all kinds of stuff we go through. The good news is that

God's love abides forever in all those who are called according to His purpose. He never leaves nor forsakes us even unto the end of age.

Does God love me and see all that I am going through? Thank God you are going through not sinking! If God did not spare his only begotten son Jesus Christ; but gave Him up to die a shameful death for you on the cross of Calvary, shed his Precious blood to justify and redeem you: then you should understand you are His beloved. Whether you believe or not, God loves you so very much. First John four verses eight says, GOD IS LOVE. So believe on this truth and accept it so you attain to eternal life. Give your life today to Jesus, trust Him and see the level of His supernatural love overflowing your life. 'It is not a secret what God can do' sang a song writer. Join the boat of the love of Jesus today and see for yourself how your life will embrace a turn around.

War Against Principalities, Powers and Rulers of Darkness.

"For we wrestle not against flesh and blood, but against principalities, against powers, against rulers of the darkness of this world, against spiritual wickedness in high places"
[Eph. 6:12]

There is need for us to discuss about the Rulers of Darkness so you understand whom you are dealing with and engage yourself wisely. Jesus said, the prince of this world is coming but have nothing in me [John 14:30].

You must not be attached to Satan in any form; he will entice you with earthly wealth/gain. If you accept his offer he will gain control over you and swallow you up but you must refuse. This will enable you fight like a wounded lion to stop his evil works against your life, job, family etc.

All who trouble you God will devour [Jeremiah. 30:16], and as you put up the right attitude to fight without fear, victory is yours!

The Principalities: These are the princes of the underworld who manipulate certain sections of this world. Satan, their master, has assigned them over nations and cities in all sections of the universe.

They function by exerting their influence over heads of nations and kings of cities, local chairmen, community leaders, etc. These demons are everywhere, even in people's homes. Every place they can find human beings. These spirits seek to control their political and private lives using them as their main device of operations. They make these leaders and their subjects to engage in evil governance. They introduce wickedness, destructive measures to eliminate lives, and make laws detriment to their subordinates etc. Good example of this is found in the book of Esther where Haman sought to annihilate the Jews in all the land of Shushan [Esther 3:8-11].

Wicked Powers: The second level of the satanic authority is the spirits in charge of decision making of cities and kingdoms, homes etc. They influence leaders in homes, churches, organizations, etc. encouraging wickedness by promoting injustice, self-centeredness, greed, controlling law makers, policy makers in authority etc. Another example of this is found in the book of Daniel when all the counselors and governors conspired against Daniel. They got King Darius to sign a decree, prohibiting all religious activities in the land. Does it surprise you when Christian activities are banned in your country or locality? These demons are responsible.

Suddenly you cannot actively participate in God's house [the church]. You give so many flimsy excuses why you cannot cope with your duty, that's it, and the demon is at work. Had Daniel complied and quit praying, he would have been killed with his friends in that land. Do all you can to stop these wicked powers before they extinguish your fire!

> *"Then Daniel was preferred above the presidents and princes, because an excellent spirit [God's Spirit] was in him; and the king thought to set him over the whole realm. Then the presidents and princes sought to find occasion against Daniel concerning the kingdom; but they could find none occasion nor fault; for as much as he is faithful, neither was there any error or fault found in him. Then said these men, we shall not find any occasion against this Daniel, except we find it against him concerning the law of his God. Then these presidents and princes assembled together to the king and said thus unto him, King Darius, live forever.*

> **All the presidents of the kingdom, the governors and princes, the counselors and the captains, have consulted together to establish a royal statute, and make a firm decree, that whosoever shall ask a petition of any God or man for thirty days, save of thee O king, he shall be cast unto the den of lions.**
>
> **Now O king, establish the decree, and sign the writing, that it be not changed, according to the law of the Medes and Persians, which altered not.**
>
> **Wherefore king Darius signed the writing and the decree"**
> **[Daniel 6:3-9]**

Demonic operations are everywhere and they conspire against God's people today mostly in godly homes and places, in individuals who had set themselves to serve God. Satan goes all the way to make things hard, make nations and people struggle, and put them in difficult situations so they deny God. Are you facing the battle of barrenness, prayerlessness, joblessness, sickness etc? Daniel stood for his God who delivered him from the lion's den. Same way stand in and hold the promises of God concerning such situations; do not lose heart and you come out a winner!

In the same manner, these wicked spirits had stopped schools and some governing counsels from praying publicly in some nations. You can take some time out to read the books of Daniel and Esther. These powers of darkness also confiscate thought patterns and feelings of most people in our societies. They influence people to kill; steal, kidnap indulge in all kinds of evil. They trap and control people's minds in a web of deception. These wicked powers make people imagine and do abominable things, slow down the compassion and concern for lost souls. They had made so many young people to be lost in the media corruption [internet fraud/ pornography]. They make you lie and believe their lies easily. They shake kingdoms, economies of countries, personal finances, presidents, governors, men, women, youths, and children etc, turning them to live evil life-style.

Rulers of Darkness: These are given the mandate of false religion all over the world. They are in control of cultic practices; they enslave souls of men in deception, false teaching, false dreams and visions. They promote horoscope, white and black magic, witch and wizard crafts, etc. they engage in attacks of all sorts to weigh people down with depression. They bring sicknesses and diseases, seating on people's mind, ruling wickedly and confusing their judgments, leading unholy lives. They multiply hatred, envy, covetousness, insecurity etc, in the lives of their victims. They energize the ungodly, oppose God's will, and frequently attack the believers of this age. They constitute a vast multitude and are organized into a highly systematized empire of evil with rank and order.

Our enemies are not natural but spiritual. We cannot win our battles if we go about it the wrong route. Some people think their fellow man is the root of the circumstances they are facing; the actual source is Satan the devil and the assigned demons to those situations. Many people tend to fight their spiritual battles with physical emotions. Carnal weapons don't destroy them but supernatural weapons that God gives do. You can't fight darkness with darkness; this is why you need Christ the Light to outshine the darkness. Your business is to call on God and trust in the blood of Jesus Christ for freedom in all aspects of your life. Our armor, as described in Ephesians 6:13-17, should be held firm, yielding ourselves to power and presence of the Holy Spirit within us as we pray.

Spiritual Wickedness: These are the wicked spirits that promote all kind of abominable sins; fornication and adultery, homosexuality and lesbianism, rape, pornography, drug addiction, suicidal deaths, other deaths. Tragedies like tsunami, earthquakes, auto and air crashes, other disasters.

These wicked spirits are really cruel and cannot be faced with party dresses or Queen's English; neither can any country's currency buy you equipments to fight them with. They are such organized wicked spirits without bodies. You are wrestling with unseen beings. Wake up my good people; take the shield of faith in Christ because these spirits operate without mercy and see you, a believer in Christ, as their worst enemy and target. Where there is light darkness has no choice because light will always outshine darkness.

John 1:5 says, "And the light shines in darkness; and the darkness comprehended it not"

The truth is that not all light can outshine darkness. For instance a tiny bulb in a hall of dark room can only be seen in a small spot area. But a big sized bulb's light covers the room and illuminates it. The volume of the light of God's Word that you are exposed to, will determine your sphere of dominance; this is to say that the actual scope of your dominion will be determined by the amount of God's Word in you. So if you want to be victorious over the forces of darkness, daily expose yourself to the light of God's Word. In the market, home, office, bus station, airport, everywhere be in the light, in your school, job and business places, be sure you are covered in His light. In your marriage let there be light, in the church too! He who dwells in the secret place of the Most high shall abide always under the shadow of the Almighty God!

Prayerlessness is another strategy these wicked spirits use to suppress and control your mindset. They make you feel you are okay whether you pray or not. They also make people to be ignorant of their devices which include envy, greed, jealousy, anger, hatred, quarrelsomeness, pride of life, lust of the flesh, arrogance, materialistic gains that tend to destruction. Beware of how you live, do not allow your mind to be occupied with the above because these demons feed on them. Attitudes like self righteousness, unforgiving are the companions of these spirits. Hide under the cross of Calvary where your solace is.

Find time dear reader, to engage in meditating on God's Word [Col. 3:16]. Many a time we read or study stuff that does not help our lives instead of studying and meditating on the Word. Some study God's word but do not meditate and act on it. Solutions to all challenges of life and what we are, and desire to be are all wrapped in the study of God's Word. Giving in to God's Word at all times will result to victorious living over the activities of the dark world. Every challenge in the day or night will have the Word to contend with if we live by it. Great men and women of God are prospering and have tremendous resounding victory through the study of the Word.

"Wisdom is the principal thing: therefore get wisdom and in all you're getting, get understanding".

[Proverbs 4:7]

They say knowledge is power and by wise counsel wars are waged against the enemy. Courageously stand in your place of authority, receive illumination of the Spirit of God, and reintroduce yourself to the Anointing of the Holy Ghost, so you can war against these manipulating forces of darkness. Keep in heart that Jesus had won this battle before now. You only connect your life to Him and He will cause you to triumph. Anointing for battle is needful. All yokes do not have choice but to quit in the presence of the Anointed and His children, the believers [Isaiah 10:27]. With the anointing you do not struggle, this is being wise.

Joshua and the Israelis fought and took over the lands allocated to their fathers by Jehovah. They drove out the Canaanites and possessed the land. This was a kind of cleansing so that they not influence the Israelis with idol worship. Daniel, Esther, David etc, all fought their ways through. Shedrac, Meshach and Abednego were courageous enough to stand against the King's order which is from the satanic world. Neither jealous insinuation of the Chaldeans nor the ugly threats of the King Nebuchadnezzar frightened them into compromising their personal convictions. Instead they stood their ground, gave bold and unhesitating witness to their only refuge and strength [Psalms 46:1].

Trust and confidence in God during times of instability, insecurity, uncertainties and adversities of life are found in God. His hand covers us during storms and dangers of life, He enables us to overcome. To overcome you must cast away fear because it is a spirit sent from hell to torment you. Satan uses it to try to keep you under his bondage. Confronting fear is the best way to defeat Satan. God has given you the spirit of love and sound mind, so face fear and deal with it courageously standing on God's word.

Dear reader, you may have gone through tough times in the past or undergoing one now, I encourage you do not lose heart or your grip on God. God is faithful and will surely shine His face on you, and then you will celebrate your victory—Amen. I've been praying and trusting God for something since year 2003; it only came to pass in 2010. Through all those years of waiting, Satan had come in so many ways and gave reasons why I won't have victory. But I kept on believing God and now I am in double celebration. Hallelujah!

Deborah sang a song of praise to God after she battled Sisera and won. God used His mighty hands to fight for the Israelis, great was the victory and that will be your portion throughout your life in Jesus name!!! When God is for you, you need not fear at all: your life is hid with Christ in God. (Col.3:3) Give Him praise for that battle you're facing now. Is it in your marriage, business, academics, etc? Believe you will experience a turnaround today. God is saying come unto me and I will show you deep things you do not know about [Jeremiah 33:3].

Repeatedly in the Bible, God had been the Mighty Man in battle, winning for His people, being a Rock of refuge to all those who trust Him. Today, God still fights for His children. I have lots and lots of victories since my walk of faith began. The enemy sought to destroy my life and marriage in so many ways, but today my home is still standing; on Christ the Solid Rock! At a time it was so difficult for my children to graduate from their Colleges, but today God had given us victory—Hallelujah!!! My faith is unshakably standing firm on Jesus Christ. He that is in me is greater than he that is in the world [1John 4:4]. He is the Lord, the mighty One in battle. Even if all hell loose, they cannot prevail because God is for me [Psalms 56:9]. This should be your confidence too! When you are confronted with challenges, stir up your faith in Him without measure. When Satan comes with his tricks, stuffing you with barriers and stumbling blocks, God is by your side making way for you. His promise says, "I will make ways in the wilderness" [Isaiah 43:19]. When the enemy is discussing your past, God is planning your future victories!! It's amazing how God plans and grants you success when your heart trusts Him; things virtually work out for you! God's righteousness established in a believer makes terror to keep far away. No weapon formed against your life prospers, and all that will gather against you shall fall for thy sake. This is a powerful promise you can hold onto [see Isaiah 54.14-17].

Hezekiah was confronted with sickness and death, as he turned to God and trusted Him for healing; God averted death and gave him more years to live.

> *"In those days was Hezekiah sick unto death. And Isaiah the prophet the son of Amoz came unto him and said unto him, Thus saith the Lord, set thine house in order: for thou shall die and not live.*
>
> *Then Hezekiah turned his face toward the wall and prayed unto the Lord, and said, Remember now, O Lord, I beseech thee, how I have walked before thee in truth and with a perfect heart, and have done that which is good in thy sight. And Hezekiah wept sore.*
>
> *Then the word of the Lord to Isaiah, saying, Go, and say to Hezekiah, thus saith the Lord, the God of David thy father, I have heard your prayer, I have seen your tears: behold, I will add unto thy days fifteen years.*
>
> *And I will deliver thee and this city out of the hand of the king of Assyria: and I will defend this city".*
>
> *[Isaiah 38:1-6]*

Trusting God has tremendous value in your life. God does what pleases you if you live to please Him and His compassion never fails.

When Jehoshaphat was confronted by three nations, he called upon the Lord, sought Him faithfully, received prophecy ". . . . Be neither afraid nor dismayed by reason of this great multitude; for the battle is not yours but God's [11Chro.20:15]. He had won this battle before this time for He said the battle is mine. This shall be your confidence. Lack of confidence had robbed many Christians their victories. Listen to me, His name is above all other names, and Satan trembles at the mention of this Name. So do not let your heart fail, because the enemy is watching out for such people. Job 3:25 says, the thing I greatly feared is come upon me. Be confident and courageous.

Gideon after making excuses in chapter six of the book of Judges, he was still used of God to deliver Israelis from the Midianites. He was courageous enough to lead his people to war against them.

David encouraged himself in the Lord and fought and won the Philistines, he pursued them till he recovered all [1Sam.30:1-8].

You can do all things with the strength of Christ [Philipians4:13].

> **Hebrew 10:35 says "Cast not away therefore your confidence, which had great recompense of reward"**

The reason why we should not cast away our confidence is that it triggers the oil of winning when we face troubles of life. It helps to know we have the Mighty God behind us assuring us that the battle is not ours. Confidence destroys the fear and defeats the devil causing us to attain victory. Show me a man who stands facing oppositions without fear and I will show you a man filled with confidence in God.

In today's world people trust in their uncles, friends, relations etc they trust in their education and technical knowhow. All of that fails; hence we have been warned not to put our confidence in man. David says, the Lord is on my side what can any man do to me. This is a true saying because life has no hope, no meaning and lifeless without Jesus in one's life. (Psalm118:6-8)

Ask Him to come into your life today and you will experience full life, victories in all life battles.

Your wining depends on what you've got in your mind. Reflection of your past victories, ways you have dealt and tackled some hard issues. These will be your strength not thoughts of how you lived in failures. When Satan reminds you of your failures, remind him his status forever in hell. Let nothing move you; let your whole life trust God for He that knows the end from the beginning knows all concerning you. Nothing past, present and future is hidden from God. He knows the number of the hairs on your head, He knows your mind, heart and can change your life if you co-operate with Him.

The tool for winning remains a receptive mind and heart towards God's Word. Paint a picture in your mind of what you want to be in life, then work on your lifestyle and pursue it diligently. Desire the best result of yourself not being passive till you get a good turnout. Love yourself and promise that you will not allow imperfections and weaknesses to stop your pursuit of your goal in life. Now trust God and follow His teachings, He never fails; He will lift you up, open your heaven of blessings, and fight your battles. The Bible says they that trust in the Lord shall be like mount Zion. The Lord is my strength and salvation whom shall I fear says the psalmist (Psalm125:1). You must not entertain fear if you must make progress. The ministry of your enemy is only to stumble and fail because God is your Light, count it all joy for surely you are a winner!

> *"The Lord is my light and my salvation; whom shall I fear? The Lord is the strength of my life; of whom shall I be afraid?*
>
> *When the wicked, even mine enemies and my foes, came upon me to eat up my flesh, they stumbled and fell".*
> *[Psalms27:1-2]*

Nothing can destroy your joy as long as you stay under the protective arms of the Master. Joy stealers and vision killers must not come close to you. Wake up as the soldier of Christ that you are and assume your position. Remember to be light and ignite light also to your neighborhood, community, state and country. Always be in the atmosphere of winning. Praise the Lord all the time for your life—Amen.

FOUR

THE HOLY SPIRIT IN BATTLE

Who is the Holy Spirit?

The believer has been destined to be the generational pacesetter for all creation. Why did I say this? Romans 8: 19 says that the whole creation is waiting with groaning and travailing in pains for the manifestation of the sons of God. This can only be possible by the power of the Holy Spirit i.e. by His operations in the life of the one He indwells. The Holy Spirit, as we know, is the third person in Trinity; God the Father, God the Son and God the Holy Spirit. He is the One in charge of the affairs of the kingdom of God on earth today and has been for ages.

God spoke into existence all the creation through His Spirit. Interestingly, nothing was created without the breath of the mighty God. When He completed the six days work and looked at it and said it is good i.e. approved with satisfaction! So without the Holy Spirit nothing can be achieved in this whole life. (Gen 1:2-3, Acts 2:1-4, Isaiah 44:3). In the days of the prophets (Ezekiel 36:22-27), God promised He will put His Spirit in you. Example of this can be found in Luke1:67, Joel 2:28

What are the works of the Holy Spirit?

In John 14:15-17, Jesus promised to send the Holy Spirit to be our Helper, Comforter (John 14:26).

The Holy Spirit helps us to pray (Romans 8:26), empowers the believer (John 1:12), gives joy, peace and righteousness (Romans 14:17).

It is the Holy Spirit that convicts us of sin (John 16:13) and leads us to repentance. He fills us with wisdom (Exodus 31:3, Isaiah 11:2)

He gives supernatural breakthrough (Isaiah 32:15). He fights for the believer, He speaks through us (2Chronicles 20:14-15, 24:20, 2 Samuel 23:2)

When the Holy Spirit indwells you, you are blessed with the spirit of boldness (2Timothy 1:7). This was the case of Peter when he addressed the rulers and elders of Israel in Acts 4:8; also Paul in the presence of King Agrippa. Have you ever wondered where you got the boldness to face the panel of interviewers in your company or when faced with danger? That's the Holy Spirit in you.

Getting the backup of the Holy Spirit is getting the anointing for battle. David was one who with boldness fought Goliath and the Philistines; even when Saul was on his neck too. With the anointing life is smooth and there will be no need for struggles.

Our victory is guaranteed in the anointing. Everything that proves tough bows before the Anointed and His anointing. Impossibilities become possible, places where you were rejected, because of the anointing, you will be accepted. All things turn out good and you become such a celebrated person everywhere you go. The Holy Spirit made the conception of Jesus by Mary possible in a supernatural way. Anointing is God's ability endowed on your ability. Anointing keeps you moving on! Fighting through life struggles is better with anointing. The truth of the matter is nothing is successful without the Holy Spirit.

a. **The Holy Spirit is called the "Angel of His presence"**
   This means that the first thing He does is to bring you to God's presence. You've got to co-operate with Him. David knew this secret and cried when he sinned that God's presence leave him not. He says, "Do not cast me away from your presence and

29

take not your Holy Spirit from me". Only the Holy Spirit can convince a soul and lead him to surrender to God Almighty.

b.   He reveals God's Word to you which helps you to live holy. No natural eyes or mind can understand the Scriptures; it takes the Spirit of God to know the mind of God [1 Cor. 2:14]. He is the Spirit of truth and will guide and show you things to come.

c.   He will bring you ability to produce Righteousness which is the nature of God. This right living will make changes in your life; business, home etc.

d.   Dynamic power will rise up within you to live above sin and overcome circumstances, oppositions of the enemy etc.

e.   He will give you rest from all wars that rise within you, all around you will be peace and contentment [Isaiah 32:17-18]. Jesus calmed the raging sea; same calmness will shield your life.

f.   He will restore, renew and refresh you. You will never run out of power or ability to achieve your desired goals. He will always lead you beside the still waters. You shall not lack [Psalms 23:1-6].

g.   He will turn your wilderness into fruitfulness. Open rivers for you in the dry and scorched land. [Isaiah 32:15-16].

h.   He will bring excellence into your life. Excellent spirit brings success. All dry bones will come back to life; fresh oil will be flowing through your veins which will radiate joy all through your life.

Every of these and more will the Spirit of God do for you. All born-again children of God enjoy His presence and they lead holy lives. Living a holy life in itself is a battle because the devil always fights believers to see that they fail, but thanks be to God who causes us to triumph over devil's wiles and temptations. Holy living and obedience pleases God.

How can you enjoy the help of the Holy Spirit?

The Bible already tells us that the Holy Spirit is our Helper (John 14:26), all we need do is allow Him take the wheel and sail our ship! He indwells every believer and manifests His functions freely in him/her. Winning battles by the Holy Spirit depends on how much quality time you spend in His presence. This enhances your growth thereby enabling you to hear and receive directions on what to do at every point in time. A casual Christian has no part possessing the Anointing of the Holy Spirit. Jesus was baptized and the Spirit of God in the likeness of the dove descended and possessed him. God said 'this is my beloved son in whom I am well pleased', indicating that His Spirit is what makes a believer to stand out and becomes a God-pleaser. The Holy Spirit is God's seal in the believer.

How The Holy Spirit Helps Us In Battle:

Who was behind the burning bush that Moses encountered? All the signs and wonders before Pharaoh and all Egypt? The darkness that covered the land [Exo.10:21-22], the Israelis leaving the land, the pillar of fire that was guiding them, the crossing of the Red Sea, their clothes and shoes not torn, the manna and the wind that brought quails; the furnished table in the wilderness, on and on . . . The Spirit of God is the brain behind all! All the battles they faced were fought by Him.

Ezekiel 37, at the valley of bones was another fight. Why do I call it fight? There are forces of darkness which will always contend with God's children through doubt and unbelief. But Prophet Ezekiel prophesied and the Wind i.e. the Holy Spirit did the miracle and the dry bones came back to life.

> *"Nay, in all things we are more than conquerors through Him that loved us"*
>
> *Romans 8:37*

Conquering is of God who loved and favored us through His Son Jesus Christ. Nothing can defeat God and the same is of you who believe that nothing is impossible with God. In other words you cannot be defeated in life because no force can defeat God. All who had victories are backed up by God's Spirit. The above Scripture reads "in all things" that is to say you can never know failure, no force can pull you down. Amazingly, God's might is made available to you when you receive the anointing. Every yoke is lifted off your life because of His Spirit.

Our Lord Jesus taught us that the Spirit of God will teach us all things, tell us things to come etc. This is unlimited access [Jn.14:26, 16:12-13].

He searches all things out [1Cor. 2:10]. When you become the lover of God you are shown things to come, He will take you by the hand and guide you into all truth; all that is to happen will be shown to you. The secret of the Lord is with them that fear Him (Psalm 25:14).

The shortest way to all that the Holy Spirit does is **crucifying self**. [Gal. 2:20]. It guarantees quick access to the Holy Spirit. Once this is done, He takes over and begins to lead you in wisdom and knowledge. He tells you of an impending battle and gives you instructions about the strategies you should employ to win. He also gives you directions in your daily living and enriches you with His fruits too! Gal. 5:22-23

> *God says, ". . . . as he who had called you is holy, so be ye holy in all manner of conversation; because it is written, and be ye holy; for I am holy"*
>
> *[1Peter1:15-16]*

Holiness is an attribute of God and it's expected of us as God's children to lead holy lives (Hebrews. 12:14). This is a sure way of having unlimited access to the Holy Spirit. Holiness carries the thought of being separated from ungodly ways of the world and be set apart for love, service and worship towards God. Holiness is the main goal of our election. It is the purpose for which Christ died that we will be like God. Holiness does not bring us to God, its main purpose is that we talk, walk, and do all things as He does. Is this possible? Yes and this can be accomplished by giving in to the Spirit of God. In Christ we receive the Holy blood infusion of grace to obey God according to His Word.

It's amazing that so many Christians have assumed holiness to be rejection of trinkets, shaven hair or do not braid at all, dressing shabbily, not taking care of the body and so on. A thousand times no, it is not at all. Do you know dirty people attract foul spirits? Cleanliness is next to godliness they say. We are admonished to be modest in our dressing. If the Spirit of God is ruling your life it shows in how you dress, speak, and conduct yourself, even in your business dealings. Some also had given themselves to gossips, ungodly conversations when castigating others and their dressings. All of these are less important. We are to be directed by His Spirit, through the anointing in our lives.

Holiness is of God, you can't stage manage it, it is the character of God. Being holy on the inside reflects on the outside. Some have chosen to talk quietly, showing love outside their homes, all in the name of holiness, but turn tigers in their real lives to members of their families. This is hypocrisy and God hates it. Some are Jezebel in sheep's clothing deceiving one's self. You are either humble or horrible and choosing to be humble is God's character.

The priority of all children of God should be to be like God, lead holy lives because this is the will of God for us. When God planned our salvation in Christ, His purpose was holiness. Ephesians 1:4 says, God chose us before the foundation of the world that we be holy and blameless. He predestined us unto the adoption of children through Jesus Christ His Son. This is why He sealed us unto redemption by His Spirit, made us new creation. God did not sight Jesus on the Cross because the sins of the whole world covered Him. He cannot behold sin in your life and be pleased. There is a whole lot the Holy Spirit can do so you are in position of pleasing God all day long.

The center of true Christian life is setting your affection above, let's read;

> *"If ye then be risen with Christ, seek those things which are above, where Christ sitteth at the right hand of God.*
>
> *Set your affections on things above, not on things on earth. For ye are dead and your life is hid with Christ in God.*

When Christ, who is our life shall appear, then shall ye also appear with Him in glory.

Mortify therefore your members who are upon the earth; fornication, uncleanness, inordinate affection, evil concupiscence, and covetousness, which is idolatry:

For which things' sake the wrath of God cometh on the children of disobedience: In which ye also walked some time, when ye lived in them. But now ye also put off all these; anger, wrath, malice, blasphemy, filthy communication out of your mouth.

Lie not one to another, seeing that you have put off the old man with his deeds. And have put on the new man which is renewed in knowledge after the image of Him that created him:

Where there is neither Greek nor Jew, circumcision nor uncircumcision, Barbarian, Scythian, bond nor free: Christ is all and in all. Put on therefore as the elect of God holy and beloved bowels of mercies, kindness, humbleness of mind, meekness, long suffering;

For-bearing one another and forgiving one another, if any man has a quarrel against any: even as Christ forgave you, so also do ye.

And above all these things put on charity, which is the bond of perfectness.

And let the peace of God rule in your hearts, to the also ye are called in one body; and be ye, thankful.

Let the word of Christ dwell in you richly in all wisdom; teaching and admonishing one another in psalms and hymns and spiritual songs, singing with grace in your hearts to the Lord.

And whatsoever ye do in word or deed, do all in the name of the
Lord Jesus, giving thanks to God and the Father by Him."
[Colossians 3:1-17]

The phrase **"set your affections on things above"** must be the priority of every blood washed believer; because you are dead [to things of this world] your life is hid with Christ in God, you must set your mind on things in heaven. Let your attitude be determined by the things above. We are to value, judge and view and consider all deeds; our life style from heavenly perspectives. Desires and goals in life should be viewed towards pleasing the Lord first. Anyone who does not put God first in life is heading towards destruction. Meeting with your Creator and securing your eternity with Christ, is priority or paramount. The material things we acquire, for example, properties, education, luxurious cars etc, in as much as they help make life comfortable, should not be our hope and confidence. Christ remains the eternal value! Life with Him here and after here should be your focus. No one will want to spend eternity in hell. Christ has prepared Paradise for your blissful stay, so seek Him. [Matt. 6:33,].

The Holy Spirit is the revealer of all hidden things. As in the case of Joseph who revealed the dream of Pharaoh by the Spirit of God [Gen. 41:38]. The heathen King recognized that only God's Spirit can do such.

In Matt. 2:13, the Holy Spirit is called the ***angel of His presence*** and revealed things according to God's purpose for our lives.

Dear reader you can see various insights provided by our loving Father to help us build a successful life and face battles of life with faith in Christ our Lord. Please use these scriptures to help you engage and access His presence in difficult times. May you experience undeniable victories as you put to work all the treasures given here in this book.

In 1998, precisely in the month of May, the Holy Spirit revealed and gave me a profound sight into my future. After concluding a church revival meeting and went home, it happened at night in a vision. I was carried into a spiritual realm and there I was brought up from a bore hole miraculously. When I woke up, I prayed handing the revelation to God. Shortly after that, an opportunity to travel to United States of America knocked at my door. Before I left Nigeria, my country home, things that I will experience during the trip were revealed to me. While there, they all came to pass. In Houston Texas an opportunity presented itself to me, I quickly went to God in prayers asking how to handle it. God answered me by revelation and I went to Braeswood Assemblies of God Church at Fondren Street and prayed thus; 'O Lord, give me wisdom to know how to go about these things'. Also I committed all into His hands and left. I did not stop praying about all that was shown to me while there and after I left States. I've been to States severally since then all to the glory of God. April 2012 marked the beginning of the manifestations of those things revealed to me back then. I believe God that open doors as regards to my life and ministry after all these years of trusting and waiting is real. In fact how it will manifest had not been my head-ache, I just focus on Him who has times and seasons in control. God's grace and mercies endures forever, He never fails!!

Wait for it for it shall not tarry [Hab. 2:3]

I shared this to encourage you and more so to buttress the fact that the Holy Spirit is the Revealer of secrets.

There is another dimension of the Holy Spirit's work that I will like to share with you. It is the ***Anointing***. When one is anointed he receives power to do exploit (Acts. 1:8). Beloved, the race you are in will catapult you to heaven. Heaven being the home of over comers indicates that you must win here on earth. To be sure you get there you must engage the One who knows how to fight, who never loses any battle. Jesus declared to overcomers 'I will make you a pillar in the temple of my God' (Rev. 3:12) i.e. interestingly; Jesus started fighting wars from birth. King Herod tried to kill Him, the Pharisees plotted against Him, satan tempted Him etc. but He fought all these destiny killers and declared on the cross 'it is finished!' Where they thought they had finished Him, there He destroyed their powers and gave you victory. He fought all the way and won all the way! Hallelujah!!! The anointing makes you live with ease, a life of no struggle. The degree of oil in you will compel every gate to open unto you (Psalm 24:7-8)

". . . . Samuel took the horn of oil anointed him [David] in the midst of his brethren: and the Spirit of the Lord came upon David from that day onward . . . ."

[I Samuel 16:13]

The anointing; At David's early stage in life, he was chosen to be king of Israel. He was anointed with oil and power was invested on him and he became a warrior. From then on he lost no battle. You have equally been anointed if you are in Christ. The kingly anointing is upon you to accomplish your destiny. The secret of David's winning life is that he loved the Lord and developed a heart and desire for God as his Shepherd from his youth (Psalms 23)

The battles you are facing now can be handed over to His hands, as you step aside, you will see warfare that will go on your behalf. You will achieve little or nothing if you fail to engage Him in your fights of faith and life. When you are in any kind of spiritual or physical fight, engage the Holy Spirit and you are victorious! In Mark 1:12, the Spirit of God drove Jesus our Lord into the wilderness where He faced Satan's temptation; the battle was so fierce that Jesus had to face Satan with the Word. You have your weaponry in the Holy Spirit who is ready not only to help you but conquer the enemies in your life, family and ministry.

Drinking or cooking meals with olive oil does not give the power. Rubbing it all over your body cannot induce the might you need either. Only when you love, seek, and choose to serve God with all your heart, not casually but in the spirit, will you get the anointing (Isaiah 55: 6, Matthew 22: 37). His presence causes the anointing to flow down on you. Anointing is costly, it will cost you your time, it will demand holy living, humility of heart, above all, loving God. You must be ready to pay the heavenly power bill.

And when this anointing comes, because you have paid the price, the heaven opens on you with favor, and all manner of blessings. You achieve success without stress, connections, breakthroughs, victories, wisdom, great ideas, knowledge, overcoming all battles; yokes and burdens disappears, all manner of suffering roll away and in due time you attain heights. Even though you are faced with difficulties, the anointing supplies you with heavenly joy to sail through.

There are weapons for conquering Satan. Weapons like unshakable faith, holiness, dependence on God, obedience, etc. When you are anointed, witches and wizards feel unsecure and lodge attacks on you without you offending anyone. But with prayer, you shall conquer all (James.5:16b), rule your world and walk in dominion!

In the late 90s, we went for a crusade in one of the rural areas of the Kaduna state [in Nigeria, West-Africa]; it was awesome what the anointing of God did. Demons were crying out as in the days of Jesus. After the meeting the chief of the town did not want us to go, he pleaded with us to continue the preaching and prayers so that their land can be saved from the attacks of the devil and demonic operations! After we closed the meeting, about ten people came for prayers for healing. The Lord healed them all out rightly. This was because the anointing of God was present to deliver and heal.

Battles against the evil plans of Satan can only be fought under the power of God's anointing. Many times people go to hospital complaining of sicknesses that sometimes medical experts cannot do anything about. Such demonic sicknesses disappear when prayers of faith are made by anointed men or women of God. No one can see the evil demonic oppression with the physical eyes or hospital equipments. I am not condemning medical expertise but such afflictions exist. Those affected run medical tests, yet nothing is found yet the sickness is eating them up still. Jesus is the answer to all wickedness of the evil one. Miraculous healings still happen today. Disciples of Jesus healed many people after the Lord's ascension and the healing ministry of Jesus flows through anointed servants of God even more in our day. There is tremendous power in the name of Jesus!

Inasmuch as the Holy Spirit does all these, His power can be under utilized in your life. This happens when you do not totally yield to His leading or not even obey his instructions at all (1 Thess.5:19, Ephesians 4:30). When this happens, the Holy Spirit withdraws because He is not forceful. Then you begin to walk in your own understanding which of course yields little or nothing. The Bible warns about trusting ourselves (Proverbs 3:5-7).

Rebelling against God's order pulled down the first anointed king of Israel, King Saul. Instead of walking in obedience he went about his own idea and failed [1Sam.15:20-23]. He was faced with the fight of gluttony spirit; he lusted after material things; even though God commanded Saul to kill King Agag and all his people including their cattle; everything was to be destroyed. (Agag is from the descendant of Haman who plotted to annihilate the Jews). But King Saul had his own ideas which led to consequences. Rebelling against God can bring rejection, displacement from your position; you can lose your God-given power and ultimately 'earn' death. (Remember Samson; Judges16)

On the other hand, David fulfilled his God-given purpose, fought Goliath and gained victory for God's people. David was a man that fought battles of all sought and came out a winner. The enemy caught him up in the web of adultery, restlessly dealt with him, yet David did not stay fallen. He rose up from his despair and cry out to God for mercy. God answered him and gave him a new life. The whole book of Psalms is an account of what God did through him and many other things he also achieved.

In 2 Kings. 9, Jehu son of Jehoshaphat was anointed king and given the mission of cleansing. He was to smite the house of Ahab, to avenge the prophets that were oppressed and killed by Jezebel. In vs 24 Jehu went ahead and carried out his mission without fear that Jezebel might kill him too. He did not stop there. In chapter 10:18-28, he further killed the prophets of Baal and destroyed its temple. He destroyed Baal out of Israel. It is only the anointed that can move with this boldness; in the face of a big challenge or dreaded person. The anointing never fails, it empowers the anointed and makes him fearless!

Earlier, we read from Colossians 3:5 'Mortify therefore your members which are upon the earth . . .' **"Mortify"** is to give tough skin to, subjugate all that will lead you to evil. Idolatry is another wicked act that God hates. ***What is idolatry?*** It is allowing money and material possessions acquired to have a place in your heart more than God

39

Himself. Many a time you hear people say "God first" yet it's not true of them. They put gold, silver, their children, properties, business, political positions, academics etc in heart more than God. Dependence on achievements and placing much comfort on them displaces reliance and faith in God. Some people are lost in idolizing images, pictures, metal crosses, statues, traditions etc. God commanded we worship no other than Him [Exo.20:3-5], He warned against the worship of graven images fashioned by men whether on earth or above the earth. They should not be bowed or prayed to or even revered. This is God's commandment and should be obeyed. You attract God's wrath when you disobey this commandment, do not even use or introduce them as spiritual help for it is abominable before God. God is a consuming fire [Hebrew 12:29].

Obedience to God's commandments attracts long life and blessings untold. God visits with favor, grace, wealth and divine health etc, those who obey Him. When God's word fills a heart richly, it is gain. Studying and meditating of the Word enriches imaginations, mindsets, temperament, deeds, thoughts, and motivations. All you do or say has to be influenced and controlled by His Spirit. It is indeed a battle to lead a holy life. This is why too many people find it difficult to serve God according to His precepts. They choose to worship and serve God their own way; they become church goers instead of Christ worshipers. Daniel would have died if he was the church going type, but his radical, unshakable faith made way for him. His holy living caused the Holy Spirit to reveal the dream of the King and also the interpretation. Living holy life saved him and his friends.

Engaging oneself in study and meditation of God's word, singing hymns and spiritual songs, admonishing yourself and other children of God gives you the energy to continue in God's presence. Watch what you say and do and who your friends are because this may be a barrier to your growing in the Lord. Growing in grace and anointing will be your focus always; obeying God's word should be your priority too. Do not be ignorant of the devil's devices. He will always seek ways to put a stumbling block before you. The fight of faith is what it is called, so have faith that God is backing you up.

Beloved, in concluding this let's examine some other weapons you can use to fight, still, with the help of the Holy Spirit. First, the Word of God; this is the sword of every believer.

> *".... as the rain cometh down and the snow from heaven returneth not thither, but watereth the earth and maketh it bring forth and bud, that it may give seed to the sower and bread to the eater: so shall my Word be that goeth forth out of my mouth: it shall not return unto me void, but it shall accomplish that which I please, and it shall prosper in the thing whereto I send it."*
>
> *[Isaiah 55:10-11]*

God's word is authentic; its authenticity has been from ages, with it He created the Universe and all that is in it. There is power in God's word; with this power in the spoken word you can recreate your world. God spoke and it stood fast. Psalms 82:6 says you are gods . . . As a child of God you can speak forth and it comes to pass. Good or bad spirit follows each word you say, so be careful what you say to yourself and situations in life and others. God's Word revives refreshes, rebuilds, replenishes, replaces, relocates, revitalizes, reshapes on and on. Go ahead, start today to use your tongue and believe in your heart, then you have it. The weapon you have to make all things new is your mouth. Isn't that awesome? God's Word is creative, it is fire, it is sharper than two edged sword (Hebrew 4:12).

Favor, graces, revelations of things to come and higher heights in this life are all stuffed in the Word. In Mathew 4:1-11, Jesus fought the devil with words and got him defeated. "It is written" is your force against the devil. All who choose to administer God's word cannot be defeated but if you choose to ignore this, the same word will stand as condemnation on the last day. It is an infallible word that catapults you into winning in life, fulfilling destiny and living eternally with Jesus in Heaven after this life here.

I will make reference to Luke 10:19 which says that you have power to silence all the powers of satan. Serpents and scorpions are terms representing the most dangerous forces of spiritual evil. You have been guaranteed victory as a believer in Christ. You can pull down these forces because your weapons are not carnal but mighty through God, to the pulling down of stronghold. (1Corinthians.10:4)

Also the Studying, meditating on and confessing the Word are good weapons in battles. When you have the word in your heart and on your lips, you will not be at lost when the devil attacks (Colossians.3:16). The Holy Spirit will through this medium enlighten your spirit with revelation by which you will gain mastery over satan's tricks. Positive confessions works a great deal in life circumstances, especially if you are a believer in Christ. Your word is never void, never be negative about what you say. When God declared let there be light, the light came forth without delay. It does not matter what situation the earth was in, at His word light came. All things shall answer to you as well . . . . Amen.

Bear in mind that it is important to be free from all accusations of the devil if you must win your battles. One common barrier is ***unforgiving***. He who must win must forgive his offenders (as long as they are humans) demons and witches must not live! Never delude yourself into thinking that you can be resentful or secretly hold grudge against someone or certain persons and still expect miracles. When we forgive our offenders, then our prayers shall be heard, healings will take place and all will be well in our lives. God is no respecter of any person; He is the Just and Truth, the only Perfect Judge.

Finally, put on the whole armor of God . . . Ephesians. 6:10-18. Be bold in the face of adversary, against all odds, be conscious of who are. Obey God's word and speak it to your situations by faith. Never put your confidence in man but in God, who never alters His words. (Psalms 89:34

─── FIVE ───

WINNING IN THE FACE ADVERSITY

What is the meaning of **adversity**? It means "trouble, misfortune, a state of hardship or affliction". The Macmillan English Dictionary puts it this way "a difficult period in your life in which you have many problems". It connotes calamity and disaster. And I add that adversity is anything that poses threat to your life.

> *But thanks be to God which giveth us the victory through our Lord Jesus Christ"*
>
> *[1Cor.15:57]*

> *"Ye are of God, little children and have overcome them: because greater is He that is in you than him that is in the world"*
>
> *[1John 4:4]*

> *"Now thanks unto God which always causeth us to triumph in Christ . . ."*
>
> *[11Cor. 2:14]*

From the above Scriptures, you can see that there is nothing to be afraid of. You have a back up through God's Word and guardian angels that are there to help! (Psalms.91:11-12) so the good news is you can never sink in the face of adversity. Jesus admonishing us said, it is expedient He goes so that the Comforter comes. The Holy Spirit our Comforter is here on earth now and helps us as we call on Him to. His job is to ensure victory against our adversaries. Jesus also obtained this victory

43

for us when He died on the cross, His blood is forever potent to deliver us from all dangers.

Psalm 27:1-3 says," The Lord is my light and my salvation; whom shall I fear? The Lord is the strength of my life; of whom shall I be afraid?

When the wicked, even mine enemies and my foes, came upon me to eat up my flesh, they stumbled and fell.

Though an host should encamp against me, my heart shall not fear: though war should rise against me, in this will I be confident".

Having seen a sure way of winning, there is need for you to brace up to face life and what it's got for you. Did you hear what the scripture said above, "they stumbled and fail" that means, each time they rise up against you, they must stumble and fall. What a powerful promise! What a decree! The good news remains that you have innumerable Angels of God to fight for and assist you against your adversaries. Do not run from the oppressor, face his oppositions boldly; the favor and grace of God keeps you moving. Storms of life should not be a threat to you; you are to face them squarely as eagles do. The Eagle is not afraid of storms. When storm comes towards it, instead of flying away, it faces the wind and flies through the stormy wind; the turbulent pressures launch it up to a soaring position. In this manner it keeps moving up and higher over the storm. You can be an eagle Christian and soar above your foes.

You have dominion over the adversities; you can rise above your troubles, live above all odds. They are under your feet, with the fire in you, you can devour all opponents that posses threats against you. 11 Corinthians 5:21 says, the righteousness of Christ had been impute in you. God also has established you in righteousness as Prophet Isaiah had said; therefore oppressions, fear and terror are far from you, Hallelujah!!!

In righteousness shalt thou be established: thou shall be far from oppression; for thou shalt not fear: and from terror; for it shall not come near thee.

[Isaih.54:14]

God also said in the following verses that surely all odds and oppositions of the enemy will gather but not by Him. The promise is that, they shall fall for thy sake! God continued to say, He is the owner of the smiths and the weapons, and that none of the weapons fashioned by the enemy shall touch you . . . Praise God! (Isaiah. 54:15-17)

How did the early believers sort out these battles? It is imperative we know that we are extra-ordinary beings and that heaven backs us up. James teaches about rejoicing always both in trials and temptations. This was the testimony of Paul and Silas. They were joyfully praising God in the face of adversity.

> *"And at midnight Paul and Silas prayed, and sang praises unto God: and the prisoners heard them.*
>
> *And suddenly there was a great earthquake, so that the foundations of the prison were shaken: and immediately all the doors were opened, and every one's bands were loosed".*
>
> *[Acts 16:25-26]*

Apostle Paul was one person who faced oppositions all through his ministry. Before that, his mission was to destroy Christians. He was a terror to them and even went on to get authority from the Sanhedrin to persecute the church at Damascus. It was on his way that the Lord captured him, dealt with him and called him into preaching the Gospel to the Gentiles. The adversary, the devil withstood him because he left serving him. The enemy frustrated his missionary journeys, brought many tribulations his way. What he suffered made him teach by the Holy Spirit,

> *". . . we must through much tribulation enter into the kingdom of God"*
>
> *[Acts 14: 22b]*

He also taught in 1Cor. 16:9, that many doors will be opened unto you but there will be many adversaries. This is true because all your potentials and talents are ready to be brought to the light if you work on them. But Satan will seek to fight you with weapons of discouragement.

For example, he tells you there is no need to put yourself through suffering all in the name of proving your potentials. God understands your children are small, you have a busy schedule, leave it till you get more time. And I ask you, when will that time be? Now is the time my beloved! You need to rise up to the challenge as long as you know God's timing. Satan makes you see your vision and dreams as pains to you if you go all out to pursue them. The reason you have not achieved your goal is because he puts you off, making the whole thing look like a futile game to you. He is a deceiver; arise to your calling now.

Do not think Satan will embrace you with love when you quit serving him and go all the way to obey God's will for your life. He will want to fight you through so many ways; work, family, even ministry, but victory is yours when you stand on God's word and revelations. Someone said when he was serving the devil, all roads of his life led to doom, [but as soon as he accepted]. But as soon as he accepts Christ as Lord and Savior and began to serve Him in truth and in spirit, all roads of his life turned to huge successes. So he concluded, Satan is wicked and evil, he only comes to kill, steal, and destroy. (John10:10)

The account of Paul's suffering makes it understandable for us to realize that God is always there for us. What he did was to stand his ground and face the odds knowing God will help him to sail through. He involved God in all and praised Him continually. Praises to God is the most powerful weapon or tool when in the midst of adversity. It causes you to be joyful instead of sad and down cast. This disappoints the devil and causes a speed-up in your deliverance. As Paul and Silas praised God earthquake was the missile God used to free them. God was the One who shook the prison foundations and got His children out (Acts.16:25-26). When you praise God, retrogression, desperation, oppositions, suppressions and all the wicked plans of the enemy and negative" ions" are destroyed. God will fill you with all the positive "ions" e.g., congratulations, desired possessions and celebrations, in Jesus Name, Amen.

Another good example of a man who faced adversary is Job. Because God was involved in and pleased with him, the devil had to get permission to touch him. (God is aware of all that goes on in the lives of His children). Job lost his children, cattle, sheep even his servants! He responded in worship to God! (Job.1:21-22). As if that was not enough, the devil afflicted him with skin disease, yet he still thanked God (Job.2:7-11). The devil's aim was to make him sin against God . . . and that is and still remains his goal; to cause man to sin against God which is why you must be careful not to fall into his trap. In the face of all these adversities, Job remained steadfast; he never cursed God. In the end, God restored him and blessed him even more than what he possessed before. (Job. 42:10-13)

We can also learn from Joseph. He was sold into slavery; an exact opposite of his dream. How could he fulfill his dream of an important personality to whom his brothers and even parents bowed? He completely set his mind towards his goal; although it was painful as regards to his brother's envy and betrayal. If he were to cry and be bitter and curse out his brothers always, he would not have made any progress. But he did not give up in the dungeon, he looked up and gradually, God brought him to the place of his dream; God's initial plan and purpose. At the end of his ordeal it all turned out well. He overcame the Pit, Potiphar, Prison and Pharaoh and became a Prime Minister in Egypt. How rewarding it is not to lose sight of your dreams in times of adversity!

For you to win, see all adversity that comes your way as part of God's instrument to fulfill your goals in life. Whether they are small or big, they are intended to help you grow in some way. God allows them to refine, purify and make you tough. They have ways of developing, equipping and building your faith towards God. If it will not benefit you, God would not allow them.

Why Does God Allow These Adversities?

The secret of your victory is the power behind you, how close you are to God and how enthusiastic you are in willingness to obey His word. When God is your focus, you are guaranteed immunity.

God allows challenges because they remind us that we are pilgrims on this earth. We are citizens of God's Kingdom; no matter how we love this earth we are going to die one day. Then the question is, are you ready to face God? [11Cor.5:2-4].

Adversities test the depth of your faith and convictions. They bring you near to God. [11Cor.1:8-9].

Adversities make you see the hopelessness and helplessness of man without God. If man is free of pain and troubles, will he remember God? [Luke 8:23-24].

Adversities are effective instruments of corrections, discipline and restoration. Generally human beings are prone to straying away from the right path. [Heb. 12:4-9].

Adversities prepare you for the final glory to be revealed in you [Rom. 8:16-18].

It also keeps you from being proud, helps you to acknowledge you can't do anything by your own power or might but by His Spirit [Zechariah 4:6].

Adversities help your spiritual growth and maturity. Hebrew 12:11 says, no chastening seems to be joyous but speaks peace for us at last. As you overcome one challenge you move up to greater heights of faith, virtue and godliness. They prepare and refine you also for your calling in ministry and life totally [Isaiah 48:10-11].

Challenges also prove your integrity. Job during such times held unto God's mercies and came out not found wanting! [Job 1:8-12].

> **He that dwelleth in the secret place of the most High shall abide under the shadow of the Almighty.**
>
> **Psalms 91:1**

This scripture expresses the security you enjoy as God's child as you trust Him fully in all.

Let's read Romans 8:35-39; "Who shall separate us from the love of Christ? Shall tribulations or distress, or persecution, or famine, or nakedness, or peril, or sword? As it is written, for thy sake we are killed all day long; we are accounted as sheep for the slaughter.

Nay, in all these things we are more than conquerors through Him that loved us.

For I am persuaded that neither death nor life, nor angels nor principalities, nor powers nor things present, nor things to come, nor height, nor depth, nor any other creature, shall be able to separate us from the love of God, which is in Christ Jesus our Lord.

Brethren, the above Scripture is clear, assuring us we have what it takes to overcome every oppositions in life. If anyone fails in his spiritual life it will not be from a lack of divine grace and love, nor from external force, or overwhelming adversity, but from his own neglect to remain in Christ Jesus. In Christ only we have God's love been manifest and only in Him do we experience it.

SIX

PRAISES, THE JOY OF WINNING

People are happy when they are awarded contracts, win awards, secure good jobs and make good grades in academics etc. All these are good and cause one to rejoice. However, the happiness derived from these can quickly disappear but joy from the Holy Ghost is ever green. It wells up from within you regardless of your status, achievements etc. This joy is our strength (Neh.8:10b).

Now what is praise all about? Praise means to express with strong approval or admiration of someone or something. Praise when given to God is worship; in words or music. Tireless praise to God gives birth to tireless miracles, signs and wonders. As your praises rise to the heavenliness, God's hands lower down to you, pouring out blessings to all areas of your lives.

Praise is lifting the Lord God for His great acts. The first song of praise was when the Israelis crossed the Red Sea. Moses could not help but open his mouth in praises and thanksgiving to God [Ex. 15:2] you also see Deborah call people to bless God for His goodness and mercies [Judges 5:2-6]. King David is another characterization of one who praised God. You too can join this wagon of praise givers to God Almighty.

In chapter 3, we saw how a shout of praise miraculously brought down the walls of Jericho and the children of Israel gained access into the city. It was God's sovereignty that brought down that thick wall. He issued the command and the people followed. Your problems can fall the same way when you trust God to do whatever he demands of you. Praise in the midst of a problem? Sounds silly right, but God is awesome. You can never predict how He works!

God usually gives specific instructions concerning certain issues. Like the case of Jehoshaphat who led the Israelis to battle in praise and their enemies were totally defeated [2Chronicles 20:15-17]. A prophecy came and he followed it and great was their victory. Jehoshaphat simply arranged singers to battle as directed and God took over the battle! Ca you imagine how God works? It is only God that can direct you to lift up a song in the midst of a war! And guess what, victory is yours if you obey.

The psalmist says, let all the people, all nations everywhere praise God. Praises to God had caused three nations to fight against themselves [IIChronicles 20:22]. Praising God always has a way of laying an ambush for the enemy. I can testify to it time without number. What causes this inner strength for fervent praises is unshakeable faith in God.

> *"God be merciful unto us, and bless us; and cause His face to shine on us; Selah.*
>
> *That thy way may be known upon earth, thy saving health among all nations.*
>
> *Let the people praise thee, O God; let the people praise thee. O let the nations be glad and sing for joy: for thou shall judge the people righteously, and govern the nations upon earth. Selah*
>
> *Let the people praise thee O God; let all the people praise thee.*
>
> *Then shall the earth yield her increase; and God, even our own God, shall bless us."*
>
> *Psalms 67:1-6*

Seeing that the battle is tense you engage yourself in ceaseless praise and praise your way through. The wise Solomon puts it this way,

> *A man shall be satisfied with good by the fruit of his mouth . . .*
> *[Proverbs. 12:14a, 13:2a, 18:20]*

Therefore satisfaction comes from the sacrifices of praise from your lips to God (Hebrew 13:15). Thanksgiving and praises to God should be a lifestyle if you want to become a candidate of signs and wonders. Continual praise to God embraces the heart of God, and puts you in your heaven of His glory. Setting your hearts on Him alone pleases Him.

Why Praise God?

There are countless reasons why we should praise God, even if it is only for His supremacy; He is the Almighty God and God above all gods.

> *"For the Lord is great, and greatly to be praise: he is to be feared above all gods. For all the gods of the nations are idols: but the Lord made the heavens. Honor and majesty are before him: strength and beauty are in his sanctuary"*
> *[Psalms. 96: 4-6]*

God created you after His image and likeness, gave you breath and you became a living soul [Gen. 2:7]. He gave you dominion to rule over all the earth. You praise Him because you are not an animal that can be killed during festive periods. Praise Him because you are unique, no one looks like you; you are wonderfully and fearfully made. (Psalms 139:14). You were originally made not evolved from an ape or fish. Human life stands higher and in a different category from all other forms of life.

Let's consider some of the spiritual blessing stored for us.

> *"Blessed be our God and Father of our Lord Jesus, who has blessed us with all spiritual blessings in the heavenly places in Christ: According as he hath chosen us in Him before the foundation of the world, that we should be holy and without blame before Him in love.: having predestined us unto the adoption of children by Jesus Christ to himself according to the good pleasure of His will,*

To the praise of the glory of his grace wherein He hath made us accepted in the beloved.

In whom we have redemption through His blood, the forgiveness of sins according to the riches of His grace . . . .

[Eph. 1:1-7]

Another reason for endless praises and thanks to God is because He chose us to be His own before the foundation of the world as you have seen in the above Scripture. Every "faithful" believer has life only in Christ. Your union with Christ is the everlasting environment you have as the redeemed of the Lord. In Christ we are adopted children of God through Jesus' death on the cross of Calvary. We are saved by grace, forgiven, freed from Satan and his co-hurts.

You should be grateful to God for your salvation; He clothed you with His righteousness, redeemed you and became your provider. He made you heirs with Jesus; as inheritors of His kingdom. All through the Bible and in your daily life there are countless reasons to praise Him. His promises are everlasting to all those who genuinely and faithfully serve Him.

Dear reader, God has already blessed you. Pause for a while and think of the goodness of God in your life, home, business, academics, ministry, and so on. Today is better than yesterday, so jump into the stream of praises to God who has provided for you. Give Jesus some minutes of dance offering and be sure you do this often for the rest of your life. David said it is good to praise the Lord at all times because he had witnessed what praises has done in his life. Beautiful testimonies and great life await true worshippers of God and all those who thank and praise Him at all times. Praise the Lord!

Titus 2:14 says it all; Jesus gave Himself for us, died on the cross to redeem us from all iniquity, totally destroyed in our lives the desire to defy God's law and holy standard, and made us holy and acceptable in God's sight. He separated us from the world and sin to become God's own possession. Peter the apostle puts it this way,

"... ye are a chosen generation, a royal priesthood, and holy nation, a peculiar people ..."

[1Peter.2:9]

Paul wrote, "Thanks be to God who causes us to triumph . . ." (II Corinthians. 2:14). So many places in the Scripture tell us the reasons for giving God all credit of what He had done yesterday, today even what He will do in the future.

Jonah would have died in the belly of the fish if he had not praised God from in there [Jonah 2:9]. Immediately God heard his thanks and praises, the fish's belly rejected Jonah at God's command. Many battles you ought to win are waiting for praises to go forth from your mouth to God Almighty.

Other reasons why God should be praised include;

God's greatness (Ps.145:3), His splendor and majesty (Ps.96:4-6), His glory (Ps. 66:1-2), His love and faithfulness (Ps. 57:9-10, 89:1-2), His holiness (Ps. 99:3, Is.6:3), His deliverance of us (Ps.124:6-8, 40:1-3). We praise God because of His acts of power (Ps.150:2), His salvation (Ps.106:1-5, Lk.2:14, 20, 1:68-75), His marvelous deeds (Is. 25:1), His glorious grace (Eph. 1:6), His loads of benefits to us! (Ps. 103:1-18, 111:1-10, Is. 63:7). Where ever you are, lift high praises to God now, His name is Marvelous, Unchangeable, Omni-present, Omni-potent and Omniscience God, He is Reliable, Undefeatable, Dependable, He is Mighty Jehovah. Let all the people praise the Lord! Make it a life-style, embrace praises to God and see how much of signs and wonders you record weekly. Undeniable testimonies are yours as you decide to key in to giving God thanks and praises, Hallelujah!

Who Should Praise God, and When?

Let everything that has breath praise the Lord . . . Psalms150.6

The earth is the Lord's and its fullness thereof, so all creation are to praise God. The trees, animals, grasses, birds, human beings and all that has breath; are to offer God high praises all the time. True praise

54

to God should not be confined to the church only. You can praise Him anywhere and anytime. Your life should be filled with His gratitude, recalling what great and wonderful things He does for you His child.

In the Old Testament, under the leadership of Moses, the Israelites witnessed God's miraculous deeds as they crossed the Red-Sea on dry ground and on foot but the Egyptians who pursued them and their horses were drowned in that same sea. They were startled on that and began to praise God. Miriam took her tumbrel and organized a powerful music concert which made all the people dance to the glory of God for their deliverance (Exodus.15:20-21). Seeing God's awful judgment against the Egyptian armies, the people feared the Lord, they thereby believed the God of Moses and His true majestic power which was revealed against sin and idolatry. Take out a time and review the lyrics of that first song of victory which they composed in Exodus 15:11, you can read the whole chapter. They praised God for delivering them from their adversary, Pharaoh of Egypt. He shielded them, became their strength, Savior, no wonder they sang "who is like unto Thee". Oh what a triumphant song of praise; the horse and the riders had been thrown into the sea!

God is worthy of our praises. He is to be greatly praised and feared above all gods. He remains the Almighty God of the entire universe. Our happiness, security, freedom and all enjoyable goodies are from Him. Anxiety, complaining and murmurings have no roots when we depend on Him. Our gratitude to God helps us to persevere daily in the face of adversity; and as we continually seek and call out to Him, our confidence grows higher, life becomes easy. He is an ever present help in times of trouble (Psalm 46:1).

The dead cannot praise God; it's the living that can! You that are alive today, praise Him. Remember that illness, auto or plane crash God saved you from. Think about His goodness, and then you see reasons to give Him all credits in your life. Call for festival of praise hallelujah; celebrate His goodness, mercies, and wealth He has given you. Praise is all I do when obstacle sets in, for in the presence of the Living Jehovah adversities are expelled one time.

Dear reader, all you are from yesterday, today and tomorrow is by the power of this great God. Your education, children, possessions, good job, high positions, degrees, built houses, name them; they all are by the grace of God upon your life. You do not get sick often and even when you do, you have always recovered. Some of your age mates have died, you are still alive, and this calls for praises unto God. Do you know how your heart, brain and blood vessels function? Do you know the number of arteries in your whole body? Can you tell how babies are formed in a woman's womb? Oh yes, I am a doctor, now can you create a life? Or stop them from passing on? These questions (and many more) make us see how great God is. All the earth is full of His glory and praises [Hab.3:3b]. His glory covered the heavens, so also His praises on all the earth. Provoke your heart to ceaseless praises, let your mouth sing His praises, let your legs find good dancing steps to glorify God at all times. Raise your hands to Him in praises if you cannot stand up; let's make a joyful noise to our God, whether in good or challenging situations.

> *"Although the fig tree shall not blossom, neither shall fruit be in the vines; the labor of the olive shall fail, and the fields shall yield no meat; the flock shall be cut off from the fold, and there shall be no herd in the stalls:*
>
> *Yet I will rejoice in the Lord, I will joy in the God of my salvation."*
> *(Habakkuk.3:17)*

Habakkuk testifies that he serves and praises God not for what He gave, but because He is God. This should also be your testimony. God is our Savior, an unfailing source of joy and strength. He is to be praised at all times; all parts of your body shall be instruments of praises to God Almighty. Your whole body is God's sanctuary; give Him high praise where ever you are. Remember also that your desire to praise God must be accompanied with a strong desire to aggressively oppose Satan's plans in your life and Christ's kingdom. Your life style of praise should be aimed at pulling down the domain of the enemy of our souls.

How To Praise God

There are no restrictions to methods for praising God. You can praise Him in your closet or in public, by singing, dancing, speaking . . . even in your native language. (Ps. 100:4, 146:1, 149:3 When you witness to people, you are praising God! (1 Peter.2:9). When you testify of His wondrous works in your life, you are praising Him. During your devotion with your family members, with your colleagues in an office meeting, at the worship service you can pour out your heart in thanks to Him to acknowledge Him. You can praise God with instruments; horns and trumpet, tambourine, etc [I Sam10:5, Ps.150:4]. Praise God for what He has done for you even what He will do in the future. Praise Him for His supremacy, mightiness, glory . . . let everything praise the Lord!

SEVEN

HUMILTY, THE MAIN INGREDIENT

"And being found in fashion as a man, He humbled himself, and became obedient unto death even the death of the cross.

Philippians 2:8

"With all lowliness and meekness, with longsuffering, forbearing one another in love"

Ephesians 4:2

To be humble means to be lowly, not proud or think highly of oneself above others. The Macmillan Dictionary used the word 'not better than other people'.

A lowly heart is a high price in God's presence. Its price is more than rubies, gold and silver. The spirit of humility wins in all. Many things go on in the mind; there, imaginations are born, and intuition, decisions and so on are made. One's destiny is accomplished more on what the mind imagines and condones. Christians are commanded to be humble in their daily lives and dealings with others. Humility is also one of the attributes of Jesus even as Lord. That's why Paul admonishes us to let the mind of Christ rule our lives (Philippians 2:5). Comparing the weight of glory our Lord Jesus left to come take up the humiliation because of our sins; gives us the perfect picture of humility. His humble heart moved him to compassion for sinners. It is important to mention that Jesus Christ has always been God by nature, equal with the Father before, during and after His time on earth. [Jn.1:1, 8:58]. Jesus Christ our Lord did not cling to His divine rights, but let go of all the privileges and glories in heaven, came to save us from Satan, sin and the world. He emptied Himself, did not mind His reputation, laid aside His position, riches, rights, the use of His divine attributes, refrained Himself from His divine capacities, accepted suffering, misunderstanding, abuses, mockery, beatings, hatred, and finally died on the cross of Calvary. He centered His life on lowliness of mind and humility to earn us salvation. He won the battle gloriously through humility.

Humility involves being conscious of your weaknesses and being disposed to ascribe credits to God and others for what you accomplish. Man is deprived creature who is sinful apart from Christ and can boast of nothing except in the Lord [Rom. 7:18, Gal. 6:3]. The Scriptures says in II Corinthians 10:17 that anyone who glories should do so in the Lord only. On your own you cannot achieve anything lasting without the help of God and others. Your worth and fruitfulness come only when you depend on God. When you humble yourself before Jesus you are doing yourself a favor. It paves a way for your destiny to flourish.

God hates pride and resists all that indulge in it [James.4:6]. It should be impressed upon our hearts and minds how much He hates it. To be proud causes God to turn from our prayers, and withhold His presence and grace from us. To be exalted in our own minds, seek honor and the esteem of others in order to satisfy our pride is to shut out the help of God. Many people are victims of these and have not made much success as they ought to have made. The whole book of Daniel chapter four deals with the result of pride; King Nebuchadnezzar was cursed and turned into beast, abased because of his pride and arrogance before the Almighty God. He lived in the forest for seven years, ate grass, and lost his throne as a king because of pride.

Humility is the absence of pride in oneself. Peter the apostle, through the Holy Spirit wrote, ". . . you are to cloth yourself with humility . . ." [1Pet. 5:5-6], he continued ". . . when you have humbled yourself under the mighty hand of God, you will be exalted in due time". Humility helps you make the world see the glory of God in your life. It helps you exhibit God's character towards others, it brings you to that level of embracing grace and mercy in your life; so you serve as Christ your example who died for the sins of others. Christ washed the disciple's feet, teaching them to serve one another with a humble heart. (John 13:1-15).

Pride goes before a fall [Proverbs 16:18], because it is connected with boasting, makes it a deadly disease. It is also connected with greed and selfishness, boastfulness. A proud person assumes that he has accomplished everything by his might. God is not in his thoughts at all hence he does not give Him credit.

> ***Love not the world, neither the things that are in the world. If any man love the world the love of the Father is not in him. For all that is in the world, the lust of the flesh, and the lust of the eyes, and the pride of life is not of the Father, but is of the world.***
> ***[1 John.2:15-16]***

It is dangerous to forget your source of accomplishments. It is also setting in for destruction, for such people the enemy can blow out everything they have acquired in a second. Pharaoh thought, in his pride, Egypt and all therein was his property, but the moment God sent Moses to go deliver His people, power changed hands. Plagues and destruction came upon him and Egyptians as God lead the Israelites out with a strong hand by Moses His servant. The straw that broke the camel's back was the death of the entire first born of both man and cattle, including Pharaoh's son. It was then his pride was sentenced, shame covered him and he lost the battle.

God says if you will humble yourself and pray, turn from your wicked ways, seek His face, He will heal you and your land. (II Chronicles 7:14) The criminal hung on the cross beside Jesus' humbled himself and said to Jesus, "Remember me in your kingdom". Our Lord Jesus saw his humility which was total "repentance" and said to him, "Today you will be with me in Paradise". This is what so many people need to do. So many people are fraudsters, adulterers, fornicators, thieves, and so on; they claim self righteousness which can never save them from the wrath of God. Why will you not humble yourselves to Jesus Christ wisely as that criminal today? Trusting in Christ will change your whole life and family. The thought of being Jesus' friend and child will create sources of strength to your whole being. Humble yourself before God and surrender completely to Jesus our Lord.

Humility Possible by Grace

"But He giveth more grace. Wherefore he saith, God resiteth the proud, but giveth grace to the humble"

James.4:6

One needs grace to be humble because man, naturally, is proud, haughty. Obedience to God's command in Christendom is made possible by grace. As long as you are willing and ready to walk with God, He gives you the grace to live a successful Christian life. (II Peter.1:2-3). I've heard people say "I believe in keeping God's commandment". No one can keep the commandments of God without grace. Grace gives you supernatural ability to go beyond your natural ability; this enables you to live the God-kind of life. A humble man receives grace to obey in all his duties and such favors him and lifts him above his peers (Isaiah. 1:19, Proverbs.3:34, James 4:10).

Let's take a quick look at what grace is all about. Read Eph.2:8-9, GRACE—*"God's Riches at Christ's Expense"*. Those who respond in faith and repentance and accept Christ as Lord and Savior receive enabling power to these riches which helps them to be regenerated [born again] by the Spirit of God. They also receive continuing grace to live the Christ-like life; resist sin, and serve God. God's grace operates within a committed believer both to will and to work for God's good pleasure. So from the beginning to end, its God's grace and grace too will enable to finish strong. Can you now see that only a humble heart receives God's kind of life? [Zoe]. This is the heart that Jesus had which enabled Him to die for the world. The force behind winning is grace. As freely given to us from God, we ought to access dependence to God, humble our lives under His glory through grace which helps us to sail through. Psalms 9:12 says, God does not neglect the cry of the humble.

Noah found grace in the eyes of the Lord, Genesis 6:8, he chose to be righteous before God. He had grace for grace. This grace enabled him to live godly in an ungodly environment and by the same grace he obtained favor to build the Ark; picked the animals, got his family into the Ark before the flood. Grace saved him and his family. As it were, the same grace applies to us today [John 1:16]. If we be available for God, we will be clothed also with grace.

Examples of Humble Bible Characters

The supreme example of humility is our Lord and Savior, Jesus Christ. Like we saw at the beginning of this chapter, His coming to earth as mere man was an action only one who is humble can take! He forsook His lordship and all the glory that comes with it, died a shameful death on earth for mortals . . . dust. He was despised, smitten, rejected and slaughtered as a lamb for mankind (Isaiah.53: 1-7). Though rich, He became poor for us to be rich (2 Corinthians. 8:9). To teach us this humility, Jesus washed His disciples' feet and asked them to do same for one another (John 13:4-5, 14).

King Ahab humbled himself before Jehovah (1Kings.21:29). His humility abated God's wrath during his reign. Humility causes one's heart to be responsive to God's word and this lead to obeying God.

In the case of Josiah in 2Kings.22:19, God heard his cry because he humbled himself and wept sore because disaster was decreed upon his land. When God sees a humble heart that trusts Him, he turns the tide of imminent destruction. This was also the case with Job who put his trust in God during his days of adversity. He repented in dust and ashes when he saw God reverse his predicament.

Isaiah the Prophet was down to earth when he was touched by the Angel of the Lord (Isaiah 6:1-6). No one becomes humble by self will, but as you repent in God's presence, He raises you up. Apostle Paul, many a time, talked about his serving the Lord in tears and humility (Acts 20:19). He was not weak but having seen the depravity of mankind and how Jesus emptied Himself to save . . . he was humbled to actualize his vision in obedience to God.

"I dwell in the high and holy place, with him also that is of a contrite and a humble spirit, to revive the spirit of the humble and to revive the heart of contrite ones"

[Is. 57:15]

This is a precious promise of the Almighty God to everyone who repents of his sinful state in humility. He seeks for hearts to revive them, personally live in them. Contrite is to be very sorry or ashamed because you have done something bad. A contrite heart refers to anyone who is oppressed by the burden of sin and wants to find freedom from its enslavement; a humble heart also refers to broken spirits due to sin and its consequence, oppressions of the wicked one, calamities and afflictions. The Lord desires to revive and give new lives to all who are willing to be free from sin and the burdens of life. The comfort of His presence radiates upon all who are under His shelter.

We must seek God while there is still the promise of His response. A day is coming when God will refuse to be found, and then it shall be late for those who reject this offer now. Therefore who ever seeks God's mercy will find it, only by humbling oneself through grace.

"The lofty looks of man shall be humbled, and the haughtiness of men shall be bowed down, and the Lord alone shall be exalted in that day. For the day of the Lord of hosts shall be upon everyone that is proud and lofty, and upon everyone that is lifted up; and he shall be brought low"

Isaiah. 2:11-12

The very serious consequence of human pride is the believing "I can decide for myself". With such dangerous decision they become independent of God, chose to live as they please. God is not obligated to people who live as they desire. His promises are yeah and amen to all who choose to serve and fear Him. In II Chronicles 7:14, God promised to hear and forgive anyone who seeks His face in humility turning away from sin. When nations, group of people or an individual recognize one's spiritual poverty and turn to God for mercy, barrenness, affliction, pestilence and all sorts of evil take their leave. If you are desperate for God's mercies and completely desire to trust and depend on Him, then

He will hear you and heal your life. Genuine repentance is turning from all forms of sin, idolatry; renounce conformity to the world and draw near to God for cleansing.

It is obvious that God will bring the attitude of haughtiness to shame and abasement; but four things will help bring revival as it were. Firstly humbling of self secondly, recognizing ones failures thirdly, manifest sorrow for your sins and lastly, seek God. When all these conditions are met, God said, He will answer and bring healing and restoration to the individual or nations. God is compassionate and will hear whoever that seeks Him in repentance. He will visit with peace, joy of salvation, truth, favor, righteousness, rain of the Holy Spirit power upon you.

There is tremendous joy when you turn to seek and please God in all that you do. The earnest pursuit of His presence, fellowship, kingdom and holiness involves hungering and thirsting for righteousness [Matt. 6:33]. Committing yourself firmly to God's will and abandoning all actions that offend God, believing in and relying on God's word as your ultimate help and confidence deepens your trust in Him. Diligence in seeking God is rewarding, it is absolute peace, well being, and has wonderful results. This is true because my life is a testimony as well and the same goes to all His faithful ones in all the earth. The battles of life are won through His abiding presence; His Spirit backs you up, strengthens, comforts and energizes you to the defeat of our foes. All who know Him wage effective war against the devil and his wicked forces without fear. I urge you to join this army of the Lord today and you win all the way. You can be that man or woman you desire when you are on the Lord's side. God is the Almighty, who has the whole world in His palm. Great are all people who accept His offer of salvation and count on Him, praise the Lord!!!

EIGHT

CONQUERING SELF, THE WORST ENEMY

To conquer means to subdue or take control of something or people by force. To gain or secure control, overcome and win. It means to be victorious! God had given us dominion and power to win. You are a winner if you desire to win today. The first chapter of this book, I explained a little about the word dominion. To "subdue" is to take authority which helps you to win in life through God's own way.

Conquering self is another tough and serious battle. I mean seriously working on your emotions, attitudes, desires, you must take charge of self if you want to and will fulfill God's purposes for your life. God had given you the power to overcome and be in charge, so failure to use this power can result in eternal loss. Therefore, take hold of God's principles through His word to fulfill destiny. You will not disappoint destiny—Amen and Amen!

Self is man's nature; what he feels or wants or thinks and we know that the Bible says man has a sinful nature (Romans.5:12, 3:23). This means that it is impossible for man to live victoriously. However, in the new life, it is possible because at salvation you are clothed with God's righteousness (II Corinthians. 5:17 . . . 1 John1:9, 4:15). In the book of Romans 8, Apostle Paul took time to explain and compare the flesh and the spirit. "Because the carnal mind is enmity against God . . ." (vs 7). "For as many as are led by the Spirit of God, they are the sons of God" (vs 14). So you see that to live above self or subject self under the spirit is a battle that must be won if you must live a victorious life.

What Are The Dangers Of Self-Centeredness?

One who is self-centered cannot please God and one who does not please God is in danger of hell! Disobedience to God and His will has cost many people their lives. The Bible teaches us to 'be your brother's keeper'. The self-centered person cares less about the next person.

> *". . . . thou fool, this night thy soul be required of thee: then whose shall those things be which thou hast provided. So is he that layeth up treasures for himself and not rich toward God".*
> *[Luke 12:20-21]*

Covetousness; it is a dangerous thing to make earthly gains and riches priority in life. It results in fatal error and leads to eternal loss of one's soul. Greed, the thirst to have more which leads to covetousness is dangerous. Am not condemning seeking to provide for your household, working hard to meet needs and be comfortable, but you should be careful least you yield to sin. While you labor for your needs to be met, trusting God will be the only motivator. We must choose to be rich towards God by seeking Him first. The above verses of Scriptures should be a warning sign for us to examine, check whether selfishness and greed is in your hearts. Satan is a manipulator; he seeks to drive human hearts subtly to destruction through greed. Greed does not mind assassinating his own in want of whatever he is out for. It is a wicked beclouded sense of living.

The "Rich fool" did not think beyond this life. His concern was how he could grab all kinds of riches for himself. again you see "self" at work. This is the dangerous thing about self-centeredness. It does not include anyone, does not feel like I've had enough, but always anxious to have some more; expand and become wealthy anyhow. The rich fool's voice went to the air; 'I will pull down my barns and build greater ones, there will I bestow all my fruits and goods. I will say to my soul, Soul thou hast much goods laid up for many years; take thy ease, eat, drink and make merry'. "I, I, I, me, me, me" that's the selfish mind you have to fight. I usually call such the doctrine of "meeiism"

The origin of "I will" is from Satan when he plotted to rise above God

"How art thou fallen from heaven, O Lucifer, son of the morning? How art thou cut down to the ground, which did weaken the nations! For thou have said in thine heart, I will ascend into heaven, I will exalt my throne above the stars of God: I will sit also upon the mount of the congregation, in the sides of the north: I will ascend above the heights of the cloud: I will be like the most high. Yet thou shall be brought down to hell, to the sides of the pit . . ."

[Isaiah 14:12-15]

In the previous chapter we considered humility which is the opposite of pride. Pride is responsible for man's desire to obey 'self'. Often people quarrel and contend for their own ideas; they always want to have their way. These are all satanic collisions pulling up their heads against themselves. Satan [Lucifer] desired to ascend above God but failed. For want of pre-eminence, he headed for rebellion against authority and great was his fall. You can now see why he rules the heart of his followers to rebel against God's authoritative Word. Have you wondered how one will forsake life and eternal bliss in heaven with Christ only to choose and prefer the ways of Satan and the world? The reason many people choose to live as they wish is Satan's idea. He wants them to spend their eternity in hell with him. He blocks their minds to the truth of the Gospel. (II Corinthians.4:4). What do you see when one is full of himself or herself? Wicked decisions that lead to evil, dictatorship, high-mindedness; arrogance, self aggrandizement, selfish interests, self-appointment, self-recognition, I deal with you languages, etc. All sorts of evil control such a life. They manifest witchcraft spirit, spirit of covetousness and jealousy and they are never happy with another's success. They are given to adultery, dubious character, competitive mindedness, they want to get all brand of cars, designer clothes, houses, the crazy women want to get all fashionable wears and under wears to seduce men; and so on. [mind you, I do not condemn having good clothes, cars etc].

Potiphar's wife is an example of such, she sought to destroy Joseph's destiny through fleshly lusts. Delilah destroyed Samson, Jezebel killed Nabaoth, and all these women are head killers. Saul the first king of Israel became full of him-self and deviated from following the Lord

God, the result was satanic seduction, envy, jealousy towards David and he was destroyed of the same evil one that seduced him. All these and a lot more are examples of what "self" does. The biggest enemy of your life is "yourself" if you are living according to the flesh. You become the greatest enemy to your success, your accelerations in destiny, fighting persons that are not fighting you all because Satan is ruling your life. You seek to be in control of everyone's breath, plans, trying to manipulate other's decisions to suit your opinion. I then ask what it shall profit a man to gain the whole world and loose his own soul. God's principals have no prejudice. He cares and loves everyone and desires you come unto Him through Jesus our Lord whom He had made the judge of all [Acts 17:30-31].

How to Conquer or Overcome self

Jesus Christ said to His disciples, *"Whosoever will come after me, let him deny himself and take up your cross and follow me" [Mark 8:34b].* Jesus Christ is the author and finisher of our faith. Looking unto Him and following his footsteps sinks all self-aggrandizement, self-appointment and self-centeredness. Arriving at all God had purposed for your life means abolishing self and all its deceitfulness. So the requirement in this context is "self denial". Denying oneself of all selfish desires and subduing the flesh is God's will for our lives. Knowing that the flesh leads to destruction, we ought to fight and win all its wickedness while we are here on this planet earth. Believe it or not, fleshly lusts have sent so many to hell and have its ugly hands on so many even now. The only way to exempt your self is subduing it and let go of its entire works. What are the works of the flesh? Let's see the book of Galatians.

> *"Now the works of the flesh are manifest which are these; Adultery, fornication, uncleanness, lasciviousness, idolatry, witchcraft, hatred variance, emulations, wrath, strife, seditions, heresies, envying, murders, drunkenness, revellings, and such like: of the which I tell you before, as I have also told you in time past, that they which do such things shall not inherit the kingdom of God"*
> *Gal. 5:19-21*

The kingdom of God is not for anyone who indulges on such things above. It is impossible for the God of holiness to co-inhabit His kingdom with sinful people. Practicing or living in such atmosphere will only lead to eternal suffering after here. Some people do say that the loving God will not put anyone in hell fire, some say there is nothing like hell. They people out there says, "If you are enjoying yourself in this life that is the heaven for you, but if not, that's hell". Be not deceived dear reader, God's word is clear in this case, and God had provided a way to all who wishes to be found in heaven and will not change His words or reduce the punishment if you neglect His offer of salvation.

The cross of Christ is a symbol of suffering, death and shame. It is ridicule, rejection, considering what Jesus had suffered in order to redeem the world. When anyone surrenders his or her life to Jesus, then you also have agreed to go the same way. This has become the very obstacle and hindering factor for many to surrender their lives to Jesus. They think it's all going to slow them down, make them less important to the society. But that is the trick of the devil so he can drag you onto his own side which is doom. Some people had chosen to be "nominal" i.e. seduced by fashion and blindly accepting nominal pleasures. They compare minimally to the real values and views of Christianity because their hearts were darkened by the enemy, Satan the devil. [Rom. 1:21].

Commitment to Christ and His cross is what Christianity is all about. On the cross our redemption started and when you take it up then you bring eternal life to your soul. Church goers have no part in the kingdom of God. Christ knows all who follow and obey His precepts and commandments. These have turned their backs to the worldly type of living and have part in the kingdom of God. Heaven is a prepared place for a prepared people.

When one is worldly, what it means is living by the dictates of the flesh. The world system of operation is darkness, corruption, selfishness; lust of the flesh, fear of unknown, robbery, murder, abortion, etc. Satan is the chief operator of this world and all his ways are against the Word of God.

The world does not see anything wrong in fornication, adultery, cheating, lying, stealing; it is not a problem to fornicate before marriage and nothing is wrong with infidelity in marriage. It's a normal life for a man to beat up his wife, marry as many women as he can get etc. They accommodate gay, homosexuality, lesbianism, and all kinds of stuff like these. Their ways are not in agreement with God's Word and can never be. Their mind-sets have gone the ways of the devil.

On the other hand God's system operates in light, righteousness, joy, peace . . . , messages of the cross, eternal life in bliss which the end result in life everlasting with Christ; on the other hand doom in the lake of fire with Satan is the world's end. So it's left for you to choose or decide how you go about it. Where you spend your eternity is up to you. When one gets born-again you migrate from the world system to heavenly system, you brace yourself up to walk in the Spirit [Gal.5:16-17], this keeps you from walking in the flesh.

The possibility of coming out of worldliness is in your hands. You can make a decision now, today and Jesus Christ who had paid the price on the cross will back you up. Remember there is a battle to fight, because Satan will not fold hands and watch you decamp and walk out on him. More importantly, you must realize that your will power cannot do this. You need to trust Jesus Christ by faith, get ready to fill your heart with God's word so the enemy comes not back again [Matt.12:43-45, write out]. The unclean spirits will not return if you fill your heart with the Holy Spirit, whom you now rely on.

NINE

KNEELING DETERMINES WINNING

What is Prayer? You must have learnt that prayer is talking to God. But it is a lot more than that. It is communicating with God; talking to and hearing from God. (Jeremiah 33:1). Our God is not a statue so He talks back to us! Prayer is a platform for renewal of strength (Psalms 84:7).

Battles of life cannot be won without fervent and earnest prayers and you need spiritual strength to pray through. There is need for you to understand the urgency of prayers in all areas of your life. Our Lord Jesus started His ministry with prayer and ended with same, how much more you and I . . . prayer is a master key! It is necessary to fit into "praying without ceasing" lifestyle [1Thess. 5:17]. The war you are in is a spiritual one, and the only type of nuclear weapons or missiles you need to win is prayer. Weapons and latest armories cannot do what God's word and prayer does. Therefore kneeling down in prayer to God is the only sure way to fight in this life [James. 5:16]. I do not mean the casual prayers you say when trusting God for money in your account. Some people's frightening moments set in when there is no money in such accounts; this is when they remember God and gasp or mutter casual prayer in fear. Some still remember God when trouble or temptation set in, and in the absence of these they do not seek God. Prayer is depending on God whether your account is fat or not!

Through prayers you exercise authority over all wicked spirits. You also claim the promises of God as you lay your hearts down in seeking Him. Connecting your spirit to God is needful in your daily life, for He alone knows all things. As your spirit knits together with His, miracles and breakthroughs will overflow your life, job opportunities, joy in the home etc. Christ Jesus prayed till He won, redeeming us from bondage of wicked Satan and the world. At Gethsemane He groaned in prayer and prayed through because He knew what He was faced with [Matt. 27:1-66]. He was sorrowful yet prayed His battle through. What can you compare with such suffering? Can there be anything you will face that could be up to such mockery, shame and death on the cross? Jesus Christ is the good example of one who knelt in prayer that lead to winning. So if our Master and Lord prayed, why can't you pray?

Mark 1:35 says, He rises up early, a great while before day, goes to a solitary place to pray. This shows that Jesus creates a good time to commune with God the Father; when there are no distractions. His ministry was a great success not just because He is the Son of God but also because He conducted Himself well bearing in mind who He is! He healed the sick, raised the dead, cast out demons. Those wonders can be done as long as you are in the place of fervent prayer. You too can perform miracles if you believe. The anointing makes the difference!!! Prayer is getting you to conform with the will of the God and not God conforming to your own will. Hence it is priority if you will have good success in life, marriage, ministry and all other things that pertains to living and enjoying everyday life.

Winning prayer

Our Master and Lord won because He humbled Himself and obeyed God the Father completely. He came from heaven as a man. Do not think there is an extra power He used. First John 4:17 says, *"As he was so are we in this world"*, He was born as you were, ate food like you do, slept, worked, went to places etc, while here on earth, until the end of His ministry, God was with Him. He suffered both physically and spiritually at the Garden of Gethsemane. Lord Jesus told His disciples to stay at a certain point while He goes yonder and prays [Matt.26:36]. He was in agony and the way to handle it is praying to His Father. He was very heavy in heart hence communicating in prayer to God who has all things mapped out for Him was necessary at that sorrowful moment. Bible recorded that His sweat was as if it were great drops of blood

[Luke 22:44]. Under great stress, the small capillaries in the sweat gland got broken and mixed blood with His sweat. Can you imagine such situation, yet He prayed that the will of His Father be done; meaning no matter the agony involved He was ready to be sacrificed in the place of sinners. By His death, Lord Jesus made provision for the removal of the guilt and power of sin; and opened the way to God for all in the world, which is "SALVATION TO ALL".

Prayer is the key to success in every area of life's battles and challenges. Moses won during his wilderness journey with Israelis through intercessory prayers. Hannah received fruit of the womb through fervent prayer. Jabez, interestingly, changed his destiny through prayers. Prayers according to God's will work tremendous miracles, accomplishing lives. You can save your marriage, overcome illness, face life battles and win them, go to great heights in life; all because you held unto God by faith in fervent prayer. Jacob's style is yet another way to gain result in prayer. He wrestled with God till his life changed. He held God and said; *"I will not let you go unless you bless me"* [Gen. 232:24-28], His name was also changed from "deceiver" to **Israel** which means "one that has power with God" Beloved, you can do a lot through kneeling down in prayer.

Abraham, our father of faith, was faced with problem of childlessness, but after a long period of time he offered a fire sacrifice to God [Genesis 15:9-15], and he got answers which was brought to pass in due season.

I often wondered what went on in Sarah's mind when she was labeled "barren woman". This is a lady married to a friend of God; a man who talks with God often and sleeps hearing God's voice all the time. What were people saying to her? Their numerous house servants and community would have wondered if her sins were so much that God had refused to give her children. For Sarah, then Sarai this was a battle of the mind.

One woman's name in the Bible was "woman with the issue of blood" and that's a battle right there. Thank God she rose by faith and the Lord healed her. But before her healing, you can imagine what she must have gone through. She could not come out in the public; she did not move an inch without her sanitary towel, she must clean herself or else she will pollute the air anywhere she went. Yeah right, a serious battle! Finally a day came she made up her mind and reached for deliverance.

Have you been labeled a barren woman, good for nothing boy, coconut head, etc, never mind just make up your mind to seek God today there will be deliverance for you. Are you being despised, ridiculed, called names, mocked for one thing or the other, go to God, cry out to Him and you will be delivered.

Bartimaeus cried to the Master after struggling for so many years with spirit of blindness. The demon of blindness left when he met the Lord [Mark.10:46-52]. Again and again in the four synoptic gospels and in the epistles are accounts of the power of God dealing with demonic forces. As long as you can cry out to the Lord, they will be cast away. Our Lord Jesus healed so many people and is healing lives till date, all by the power of the Lord God Almighty. Restoration can take place when we pray. All our requests are to be made known to God [Phil.4:8].

Elijah prayed and fire came from heaven and consumed the sacrifice in the presence of King Ahab and the prophets of Baal [1Kings 18:36-39]. He consumed his arresters with fire through prophetic prayers. Fire came from above and killed the captain of fifty soldiers at the word of the man of God, which means he consumed his enemies by fire! [2 Kings 1:1-14]. What you see in the lives of numerous men and women of God today is as a result of prayers. You cannot neglect prayers in the midst of wars and difficulties in the world today and you cannot neglect it in your time of success either. Those that neglect prayers do not understand the power therein. There are people that have the attitude of whether I pray or not things will still work out for me. It's okay but the fact that God works it out calls for thanksgiving to Him in prayer. Prayer is important.

To enjoy God's intervention, open doors and accelerations, higher heights, win battles, sustain your miracles, etc; prayer should be an important aspect of your life.

Winning prayer is to make decrees. Decree a thing and it shall be established [Job. 22:28]. Asking is very important; A.S.K according to Matt. 7:7, when you ask, seek and knock the door will be opened to you. The reason some people do not get results is because they ask amiss; to satisfy their evil desires. When your motive is wrong, do not expect answers. God intervenes to the point of causing nature to comply with you when He sees your sincere motives. Joshua prayed and the sun stood still till he finished his battle against his enemies. What an honor to have God alter nature for your sake! [Joshua 10:12-14] God knows all things, sees all hearts, when we are serious or not He sees. You have to mean business in prayer to God not giving the sacrifices of fools.

Why Should You Pray?

In reference to what prayer is, you should pray to commune with God; in prayer you receive instructions or directions or revelations about something/circumstance. Through the books of Moses, we see how God instructed him on how to carry out certain assignments; from speaking to Pharaoh , to leading the Israelis through the wilderness, anointing Aaron and his sons, building the tabernacle etc. [Ex.3:14, 4:21, Lev. 6,8,10 . . .) God deals differently with individuals and gives specific instructions for specific things. He taught David's hand to war, Noah's to build an ark and Aaron's to discharge priestly duties. The apostles' walk with God in the New Testament all point to hearing from God.

Through prayer we renew our trust in the Lord's faithfulness by casting our anxieties and problems upon Him who cares for us [Matt. 6:25-34, 1Pet. 5:7]. The peace of God guards our hearts and minds as a result of our communion with Christ [Is. 26:3, Col. 3:15]. God strengthens us to do all things He desires of us [Phil. 4:13, Eph. 3:16]. We receive mercy, grace and help in times of need [Heb. 4:16]. We are assured that all things God allow to happen to us will work out for our good [Rom. 8:28]

Without prayers, one can fall victim of Satan's numerous vices. His hidden agenda and schemes are too many. He is after your downfall, constantly planning evil against you. He plans evil to stop your destiny from taking shape and fulfilling God's purpose for your life. He wants to cause you violate God's order and question His authority. He never wants to see you serve God effectively; his greatest plan is to keep you from accepting the offer for salvation which is provided for you. Satan does not want to see your success; he wants to frustrate your job/career, academics, marriage, ministry etc. In some cases he possesses people and causes them to make wrong decisions that ruin their destiny (ies). The devil's ministry is kill, steal and destroy (2 Peter 5:8, John 10:10).

A deliverance minister found out while carrying out his work, that there were demons following a man influencing and causing him to quit his job unnecessarily. His life became a mess and came to a standstill. No progress, his family suffered hunger and all kinds of pains. But shortly after his eyes were opened through God's word he knew it was satan's vice to confuse and destroy his destiny. He was prayed for and delivered from those shackles.

Take some time and read Matt.12:43-45, you will see why you need to pray. Have you not seen where a whole village is taken by some demonic forces and as such immoral living is welcomed? They go to extreme to do all kinds of evil, yet they see no wrong in doing them. Some people's marriages are delayed and in some cases, totally cancelled. Some others experience delays when it comes to bearing children. The cause being that they have demonic imprints on their faces, which repels, instead of attract the opposite sex. Other reasons include spirit spouse, generational curses, etc. In the scripture above you see that demons possess people, after they are cast out, they roam around for a new abode but when they cannot find any, they return to the former if they find it unoccupied. When God's word is not in the person's heart and he is not praying to maintain his deliverance this is the result. Now you can see that too many human hearts had been possessed that's why you see all kinds of evil characters ruling people's lives. Some manifests anger outrageously, causing damages in relationships, at job places, some seek to control everybody's affairs, dictate and impose their lifestyles to others, and all kinds of things go wrong with such demon controlled humans. He causes some to invest wrongly putting their money in businesses that do not yield dividends.

When prayers in Jesus' name are made, these wicked satanic forces are dealt with, they bow and people are set free. If Satan would tempt our Lord Jesus, tried to stop His ministry, then he cannot spare you mortal man! [Matt 4:1-11]. Cases as those can only be treated by enacting deliverance, and bind Satan in the name of Jesus. We are in a real war, and as soldiers we must be alert. We are to cast out, disarm demonic forces of all levels. Our weapons are mighty [1Cor.10:4]. We are to resist the devil, tread on Satan and his demons. Our Lord gave us power to trample on serpents and scorpions i.e. satanic and demonic forces, it is then our duty to exercise dominion over them and they shall by no means hurt us. Aggressive prayers made in faith and power, flush out demonic plans in lives of their victims.

> ***Psalms 34:17 says, "the righteous cry, and the Lord heareth and delivereth . . ."***

Are you in any kind of battle right now? There is hope for you! The righteous are those that obey God's will, who stand strongly in faith; they are committed and ready to follow the demands of living a holy life as required of believers saved by grace. They are under the coverage of God's grace and mercy—they dwell in the secret place of the most High, and abide under the shadow of the Almighty God. In storms of life they press on, even when family members turn against them; yet they move on. All battles of life are 'cheap' for them, when they pray God hears and shows them great and mighty things they do not know about [Jeremiah 33:3]. Crying to God changes situations, brings deliverance, healing, success, accelerations, retains the glory and increases joy of living without stress.

The place of crying is a place of prayer; a serious agonizing prayer avails much. This kind of prayer scares demons because it oozes out fire. That was the kind of prayer Elijah drew down that licked all the water in the trench of sacrifice in his day in Israel, and there after the rain fell. Job puts it this way, ***"There is a path which no fowl knoweth*** . . . no demon can perch on such fire filled prayer [it is called fire for fire], the satanic forces are roasted by it. This is where the believer in Christ settles all problems. Cancerous diseases and terminal sicknesses dry up in the presence of fire packed prayers. On your knees mighty things happen! When you mix it with whole hearted offering to God, doors open on their own accord. The church said this kind of prayer and the angel of God released Peter from the prison [Acts 12:5]. It is important to mention that you must be bold in prayer, not timid. Pray to get your deliverance, fulfill your destiny and live a fruitful life on earth.

How to pray

In Luke 11:1-4, Jesus taught us how to pray. You must come before God acknowledging His mightiness and supremacy. You must hallow His name; to hallow is to treat with great respect, to consider as holy. In prayer you can ask God for your well being, daily bread, ask for mercy and pray against temptation. When praying, you can employ the different types of prayer depending on what you have before the Lord with. We shall consider these briefly.

> *"I exhort therefore that first of all supplications, prayers, intercessions and giving of thanks, be made for all men; for kings and all that are in authority ; that we may lead a quiet and peaceable life in all godliness and honesty"*
> *1 Timothy 2:1-2*

There is the prayer of thanksgiving. David prayed a lot of this. In thanksgiving you express gratitude for God's goodness unto you [Ps. 100:4, 1Tim.4:4, II Cor.4:15]. Prayer of petition and supplication where your requests are made to God [1Sam.1:17, Esther5:6, Phil.4:6, Eph.6:18]. Warfare prayer; you wage war against the enemy and reject his vices [Isaiah 49:24-26, Lk. 10:19]. Prayer of intercession; prayers are offered on someone's behalf like Jesus always prays for us! [Heb. 7:25, Rom. 8:27, Jer. 7:16]. Prayer of agreement, here you join your faith with another person or brethren. [Matt.18:19].

Pray till you see results, till heaven opens on you, till something happens!! I have lots and lots of enviable testimonies as a result of holding unto God in faith through prayers. When you pray use the Word of God, that way you are praying according to the will of God. The word of God works tremendously; sometimes it may seem that you are not getting answers, just hold fast. [Habakkuk2:3]. Believe you have received, continue in thanksgiving, it shall manifest.

We can use the method of *fasting and prayers* i.e. waiting on God. Someone may ask, does a Sovereign and all powerful God need our involvement or not, is praying and fasting important? Yes it is important to build you up, help to raise your faith and courage towards God for help. One thing is certain, you cannot do without God in your life, and only in Him we have answer to life. Man's dependence is on Him; outside Him we cannot achieve anything. The disciples of Jesus at one time could not cast out demon from a boy, He explained to them His disappointment towards their unbelief and urged them; they need to indulge in fasting and prayer to achieve results. [Matthew 17:14-20].

Fasting and praying is giving yourself to the worship of the Almighty God. When you exempt from eating and drinking or some pleasures and comfortable times as a sacrifice to lift others up in prayers, do you not see that it is pleasing to God? Fasting helps to rebuild your christian life, helps you apply discipline and self-control in times of challenges. It also helps you to refrain from sin that easily beset you such as; gluttony, over sleeping and relaxation which endangers you to the enemy's defeat. Fasting and praying produces favor, divine health, graces to rise up to challenges.

Queen Esther was set to go into the presence of the King at the odd season because she and her maids fasted and prayed. God answered her prayers and reversed the annihilation that was earlier decreed for her people [Esther 4:16].

Jehoshaphat also proclaimed a fast in his days when the army of three nations came against him. As they prayed God came to their rescue. God specifically said, if you humble yourself and pray He will forgive sins, and hear and heal the land [or home] anything you pray for. It's a promise you need to queue into [II Chro. 7:14]. God will take over your battle if you invite Him through humbling yourself in fasting and prayer. I am a witness to God's faithfulness on such issues. With my dependence on Him I smile all day long. I can boldly confess our LORD GOD IS FAITHFUL!!!!!!!

It can never be overemphasized the way God works miracles when you involve Him in your daily life and situations. In Joel 2:12-17, the people fasted and prayed and godly sorrow that leads to repentance was the result. In Acts 13:2-3, we see how Spirit filled believers were led to make good decisions. Full acknowledgement of God's power through fasting and prayer restores, revives, re-freshens, does well to nations, group of people, individuals, heals and delivers from evil. It causes signs and wonders of God to visit the earth.

What Makes Prayer Effective

Please understand that kneeling is not the only position you can take to pray. You can stand, sit or even lie on your face but be sure it is effective.

> *". . . the effectual fervent prayer of a righteous man availeth much".*
>
> *James 5:16b*

> *"The sacrifice of the wicked is an abomination to the Lord: but the prayer of the upright is His delight. The way of the wicked is an abomination unto the Lord: but He loveth him that followeth after righteousness".*
>
> *Proverbs.15:8-9*

Righteousness makes prayer effective. God detests the prayer of a sinner but listens to that of His child. It is he who has a pure heart and clean hands that can ascend to the hill of the Lord (Psalms 24:3-4, 66:18). Live in the fear of God; do not allow strife be found in you. Forgive those who have wronged you (Mark 11:25-26, Luke 17:3, Matthew 6:12). Unforgiving is a sin. Prayer should and must be said in the name of Jesus. John 14:13-14 says, *"Whatsoever ye shall ask in my name, that will I do . . . ."* This means two things; firstly you pray in harmony with His person and secondly pray with faith in Him, and in His authority with the desire to glorify both the Father and the Son. This way our Lord Jesus will honor any prayer that He would have prayed Himself. There is no limit to the power of prayer when addressed to Jesus our Lord or the Almighty God in faith according to His desire. Prayer according to God's will is effective, it is answered 1 John 5:14

Persistent Prayer [Luke 18:1-7]

Our Lord Jesus taught us to pray always and not to faint. Praying frequently and continually should be priority to you. It helps you to accomplish God's purposes [Jeremiah. 29:11-13]; God knows what He has in stock for your life. Seeking Him and being persistent in prayer brings such plans to pass. From the persistent widow in the scripture above, we see that persevering is key. This is a great virtue and should be used in all matters of life even unto the return of our Lord. We have an adversary who does not go on break, so you too must persist in righteousness till He comes back to take you home. It is also important to know that our adversary Satan the devil is roaring like a lion seeking whom he may devour. [1Peter 5:8]. God's true elects should not relent in seeking and praying to Him. The admonition in verse seven of the scripture above is that God will avenge His people who cry out day and night. They will persevere day and night, at any moment of the day. My experience of singing worship songs, even when I am working in my kitchen saved my family from satanic arrangements some time ago. The lady in question confessed that my songs carry fire and do not allow her fly out to their demonic meetings; thereby caused their wicked agenda to flop. In your car and homes play godly music, it scares the devil a whole lot! Thanksgiving for all we have asked is one way to persist in prayer not repetitions. Once you make your request God hears, all you do afterwards is to praise Him for your Answers. ***"Now unto Him that is able . . . . [Eph. 3:20],*** God is able to deliver, mighty to save, liberate, put an end to suffering or persecutions, distresses, challenges etc, when you seek Him earnestly in persevering prayer. He does more than you can imagine and think!

As you pray, steadfastly resist the devil and do not doubt in your heart for he will want to afflict you with his poison of unbelief. To be steadfast means to be strong willed, persistent and fervently keep watch; being spiritually alive, awake or alert. Sensitivity, devotion, and unshakable faith with hope will enhance your winning. Be informed that Satan and the weaknesses of human nature will attempt to cause you to neglect your duty. Distractions also will force you out of the arena of persistent prayer, so be alert to the nudges of the Spirit of God. Have a good mind-set; discipline of self is also required to achieve victory, because Satan and the pleasures of the world must set themselves in array to fight you.

Decree as follows,

> *"I am born of God; I have my origin in God. I am sanctified by the Blood of Jesus therefore I am a winner in Christ Jesus. I live in dominion and have overcome the world. I have authority over the elements and principles of this world! God's kind of life [Zoe] operates in me, therefore I am indestructible. The imperishable life in Christ is mine and this life knows no sickness, disease, defeat, failure, sorrow, etc, because of this life I reign in this earth as a king and all wicked operations of the devil are under my feet! I decree that I am a champion as the Word of God has said concerning me. The Bible declares concerning me that I have received abundance of grace and of the gift of righteousness and reign with Christ [Romans 5:17]. So I know who I am! I have found my roots and as Jesus reigns so I reign in this life. I decree health is mine, prosperity is mine, divine life is mine, I had been vitalized by the Blood of Jesus; so as He never gets sick, so also I am healthy, it is well with my soul all the way, in Jesus Name I decree . . . Amen!"*

Power packed declaration prayers as above gets the devil mad and carries Holy Ghost fire to his domain. He knows you know who you are in Christ yet tries to lie to you. David in Psalms says God teaches our hands to war and our fingers to fight! In other words create words using the authoritative word of Almighty God which breaks barriers!

Do you need a miracle, then be happy because you are in charge if you are in Christ Jesus. Rejoice always in the Lord, recalling God's grace in your life, always remind yourself of His nearness and promises; allowing joy to fill your heart. Be not anxious or worried for anything. The one essential cure for worry is prayer.

I have learnt how to queue myself to this verse of the scripture, "all things work for my good" [Rom. 8:28], believing that God had planned my life even before I was born into this world. All our endeavors has to be given to Him who already knows the end from the beginning [Isaiah 46:10]. If you are a Bible scholar you see God telling the major and Minor Prophets what will come to pass in the land of Israel before time. So put your life in the hands of the Master and it shall go well with you.

Finally dear readers, place your mind on those things which are true, pure, holy, righteous, etc. All these are the prerequisite for experiencing the peace and favor of God; freedom from anxiety and all that is evil. Remember that the consequences of placing your heart on unholy things of the world will rob you of God's presence and its benefits. So what do you do? Set your heart and mind to those things above and let your attitude be determined by the things above [Col.3:1-4]. Value, judge, view, and consider everything from an eternal and heavenly perspective. Shun sin, reject the world system, pursue your goals, dreams and all your ambitions with the character of Christ; seeking spiritual graces, power, promises and all God's blessings which lead to everlasting life in God's bosom. Our Lord Jesus prayed at the cross, "It is finished" this means that trusting Him brings our lives to the place of winning life battles.

I decree to you that you have won! You are blessed!!!!!!!!!!!

---- TEN ----

THE TURN AROUND EXPERIENCE

"And Jesus entered and passed through Jericho. And behold, there was a man named Zaccheus, which was the chief among the publicans, and he was rich. And he sought to see Jesus who he was; and could not for the press, because he was little of stature. And he ran before, and climbed up unto a sycomore tree to see him: for he was to pass that way. And when Jesus came to the place, he looked up, and saw him, and said unto him, Zaccheus, make haste, and come down; for today I must abide at thy house. And he made haste, and came down, and received him joyfully. And when they saw it, they all murmured saying, that he was gone to be guest with a man that is a sinner. And Zaccheus stood, and said unto the Lord; Behold Lord, the half of my goods I give to the poor; and if I have taken anything from any man by false accusation, I restore him fourfold. And Jesus said unto him, this day is salvation come into this house, for so much as he also is a son of Abraham. For the Son of man is come to seek and to save that which is lost"

[Luke 19:1-10]

Every one desires to be wealthy in physical riches, how about *the* spiritual riches? Many a time people's thought would be that the gospel is for the poor because it is not popular. Here Zaccheus had shown that the Gospel is not for the poor only, but for the rich also. Often time people think that commitment and faith towards Christ is for the lower people [not well to do] in the society. All people are in need of Christ both poor and rich. This will definitely admonish us to bring the

Gospel to the socially undesirables of society, for the world is lost and in need of Christ the Savior.

The tax collector and rich man of his day received Jesus with joy [vs6] in the above scripture. Folks, if you are too big for repentance then you are too big to be saved through God's grace. He made up his mind and decided to give up Jesus for you, would you not make use of this opportunity? Climbing the tree even though he is a rich man showed that Zacchaeus was in dire need of salvation. He restituted all he gained falsely and welcomed the Lord in his home i.e. his heart.

In John 5, the Bible tells of a certain man at the pool of Bethesda who suffered an infirmity for thirty eight years. He probably has been there for that long too waiting to get healed when the pool is stirred by the angel. But when he came in contact with Jesus Christ, he did not need to get in the water anymore. Jesus healed him and his story changed.

Another man, born blind met with Jesus and the blindness became a thing of the past. He testifies thus 'once I was blind but now I see'. What a miracle! [John.9]A certain widow whose son was dead had her boy raised back to life. [Luke7:11]. Her hope was restored. This boy's destiny had been hit but a turnaround blessing brought victory to the family. In Luke 13:11-13, a bound woman was loosed from an eighteen years infirmity, she went home rejoicing! Everyone who came in contact with Jesus experienced a turnaround in their lives. A song writer wrote 'anywhere Jesus went He was doing good . . . even today, he is still doing good!'

Naaman, the captain of Assyria army got healed after he obeyed Elisha who asked him to go and dip seven times into River Jordan. For his sick skin he got a new one; like that of a new baby [2Kings.5:1-14]. Apostle Paul's conversion was a massive turnaround. One who once stood against the kingdom of God and His word and oppressed believers became a preacher to the Gentiles. His encounter with the Lord on his way to Damascus ushered in his salvation, healing and into actualizing the destiny God ordained for him. He wrote all the epistles and served God to the best of his capacity.

Why is conversion to Christ very necessary?

"Jesus answered and said unto him, verily, verily I say unto thee, except a man be born again, he cannot see the kingdom of God"
John 3:3

"Jesus said unto him, I am the way, the truth, and the life: no man cometh unto the Father, but by Me"
John 14:6

Salvation is through acceptance of the sacrifice of Jesus Christ on the cross. Repentance of sins, faith and believe in Christ and commitment to God. "YOU MUST BE BORN-AGAIN" and this is the work of the Holy Spirit [John 3:3]. You do not need to know how God works it out, only trust Him for the turn around. It is not something you can figure out. Can you figure out how you came into being? What substance were you made of? Do you know what substance the air you breathe in contains? Can you measure the sea and the oceans; certainly you do not know how God moves.

Surrendering to God is the first step, when you do; you pass from death to eternal life in a moment. It is an instant miracle; the life of God [Zoe] becomes yours and supernaturally you are lifted to God's level of life. You have no life till you experience Christ.

Romans 3:10-11 says, "No one is righteous, no one seeks God . . . ." The deplorable condition of mankind continues because "there is no fear of God before their eyes". If there had been the fear of God, they would have sought reconciliation and peace. Only by the fear of God can man depart from evil and have peace [Pro.16:6]. As long as man runs away from God, his heart will continue in darkness. The result is wickedness, corruption, deceit etc. and all these are from the heart of man where feelings and thoughts proceed. This corrupted human heart cannot change by itself, the remedy is to experience God's grace, become renewed [born again] through faith in Christ and receive a "new heart", one that hates evil and delights in doing God's will [Ezekiel 36:26-27].

Romans 3:23 says "all have sinned . . . 6:23 says "the wages of sin is death . . ." Can you imagine the danger you're in, if you have not made Jesus Christ your Lord and personal Savior; if you do not live to please Him, and look towards the final salvation which is the resurrection of the saints [Rapture]. Apostle Paul also pointed out that your only ground of salvation and righteousness is Jesus' sacrificial death and shed blood on Calvary. Your utmost desire as a runner in the heavenly race should be, pressing forward with an intense concentration in order not to fall short of the goal that Christ had set before us.

God promises to restore every heart that responds to His word. He promises to put His Spirit within their heart and help them live according to His will. The men and women throughout the universe who desires to live for Jesus are pleasing to God. They are a called out people [believers in Christ] willing to lead holy lives and serve God whole heartedly according to the dictates of the Spirit of God. You may ask how that can be. The grace of God [acceptance of Christ's death for you] leads a man to please God.

At both sides of Jesus on the cross, two men were hung up. One received this grace there and then when he asked Jesus into his life. He was promised Paradise immediately because Christ's death is for him too. He saw the fountain of cleansing [the death of Christ], the blood that can take his sins away. Remember both of them are condemned to death like you and I, but one quickly gave up "self" crucified his flesh and headed for Paradise instead of hell. He knew in the few seconds he will be heading for destruction, so he turned to Jesus requesting mercy from Him. He obliged and freed him. What a wonderful Savior!! The thief was a smart guy, he tapped into eternal life.

When Jesus said "it is finished" the whole world was freed of the punishment of sin. It is left for you to accept that your sins are done with on the cross, and you will be saved.

Let me use this opportunity to talk about hell. Hell is a place of unquenchable fire, it's so terrible. It is the destiny of the lost souls, all who reject God's offer of salvation. This means as many as do not accept Christ's death and His teachings, those that lived as they pleased, rejected God's grace and mercies will not enter God's kingdom. So every influence of sin must be opposed and rejected whatever it costs you so that you can make heaven.

> *"And I saw the dead, small and great, stand before God; and the books were opened: and another book was opened, which is the book of life: and the dead were judged out of those things which were written in the books, according to their works. And the sea gave up the dead, who were in it, and death and hell delivered up the dead who were in them, and they were judged every man according to their works. And death and hell were cast into the lake of fire. This is the second death. And whosoever was not found written in the book of life was cast into the lake of fire".*
>
> *Revelation 20:12-15*

The example of Zacchaeus coming to Christ is what many people on earth need today; it shows the necessity of salvation. Remember he became rich through fraud, cheating on people's taxes, a popular tycoon, of a high class in the society, one who had been living on dishonest gains, yet he saw the need to repent, confess his sins to Jesus and turn over a new leaf. Only through confession [not to any priest], but to Jesus and genuine faith saves. The determination or decision should well up from within your spirit; this is only when flesh is subdued. The change is in the heart while the outward manifestation is holy living. It is an interesting thing to share Christ's life and walk with Him. A turn-around experience is needful. Our lifestyle must center on what God desires for us as His children. A life of rest in God and His Kingdom! Be warned God cannot lower His standard for anyone. He expects you to come up to His righteous standard. God is no respecter of persons but judge according to His word; gives grace unto all who seek Him.

Dear reader, strive to make heaven your eternal home after here. You will not miss out. It is a place of bliss, rejoicing in the presence of God where all who served Him obediently and effectively shall rejoice forever. It is a place of feasting and joyfully raising songs of the victorious, where there is no weeping or crying, nor pain, and sorrow shall not be there at all [Rev.21:4]. Heaven is full of enjoyment. You do have sorrows and pains here on earth mixed with happiness sometimes. Heaven is joy, joy, joy, no presence of evil, pain sorrow, demonic attacks etc. see what I mean? Heaven is indescribable; nothing can be compared to the glory reserved for all who love and walk with Jesus Christ. It is experiencing God in His totality. All who have denied themselves the so called worldly enjoyment will live there forever and ever. Hallelujah!!!!!!!!!!!

Now, with the little knowledge of heaven and hell you make your choice and decide on where you will spend your eternity, this is the greatest battle you will ever face. This is because all human beings will live forever either in heaven, if you accept the offer of salvation, or in the lake of fire that burn with brimstone if you reject salvation in Christ. It does not matter the color your sins, black, blue, red, dark-red, whatever. God says, come as you are, let's reason together.. [Isaiah. 1:18] I do not care if you are the worst sinner, hypocrite, adulterer, liar, whatever you think you had been in, come [Matt. 11:28-29]. Are you a witch or wizard who sit in the coven all day? God says come. You will not regret ever coming to Christ.

Burdens are lifted at Calvary, deliverance, liberty, freedom is only found in Christ Jesus. The indwelling of the Holy Spirit helps you live as God wills in Christ. Do not forsake this great moment of change in your life!

See for yourself what God has in stock for you. you are blessed as you do, Praise the Lord. Hallelujah!!!!!!!!!!!!!!!!!!!

DECISION STATEMENT

Jesus Christ my Lord, I believe You died for me, shed Your blood on the cross for my forgiveness. Today, Dear Lord, please forgive all my sins, cleanse me from all transgressions and free me from the bondage of satan and sin. I receive You into my heart today as my Lord and personal Savoir. Help me with Your Spirit to abide in You. Heavenly Father write my name in the Lamb's Book of Life. Thank You for saving my life, amen.

Congratulations! You are now born again. Your own turnaround experience has just begun. Welcome to the family of God!!!

BREAKTHROUGH PRAYERS

Below are some break-through prayers I gave some of my children when things were rough precisely October 2011. After declaration of these power packed prayers with the Word, they got their controversial testimonies. If you would you can pray this:

Father in the name of Jesus, I come before you with thanksgiving, praises and worship. I adore you my loving Heavenly Father for your Hands of mercies and favors upon my life. Thank You for drawing me to you through faith in Jesus Christ's cleansing blood. You are the joy of my life, you are my anchor, and you are my fortress. You are beautiful in all my situations. Mighty God, receive all adoration and thanks in Jesus name amen! [Sing songs and worship God with Psalms 100, 118, 150].

Father, You said in Jeremiah 29:11, ". . . I know the thoughts I think towards you, thought of peace not of evil, to give you an expected end . . ."

Almighty God, therefore, I decree that my life is hid in Christ with you [Colossians 3:3], I am an over comer [1John 5:4], and covered in the blood of Jesus, and I confess that I must enjoy life and prosper in all areas, and it is happening now . . .

Your plans of physical and spiritual prosperity for me must come to pass
Your plans of good harmonious marriage for me must come to pass . . .
Your plans to give me success academically must come to pass . . .
Your plans to give me good job must come to pass today . . .
Your plans for me to bare my own children must come to pass . . .
Your plans for me to cherish my family must come to pass . . .
Your plans for me to always radiate your glory must come to . . .
Your plans for me to be fulfilled in life and ministry must come to . . .

Your plans for me to be in divine health always must come to . . . .
Your plans for me to reach the heavenly home must come to pass . . .
Your plans for me to fulfill all life purposes must come to pass . . .

And so on . . . .

Therefore, with the Holy Ghost fire I decree that I am not going to fail and can never be a failure. I throw out to desolation all low types of living such as, discouragements, disappointments, fear of the unknown, depression, suppression, oppositions, frustrations, fake miracles, fake husband, fake wife, fake solutions, and fake hopes, unfriendly friends, doubt, unbelief, spiritual blindness, demonic ministrations, violations and abuses in the dream, consequences of broken evil covenants, witches and wizard oppressions, hindrances and potholes, and so on . . ., let them all roast by fire with their wickedness [Isaiah 49:24-26, Jeremiah 30:16].

With Holy Ghost fire I visit my paternal and maternal foundations; I destroy all wicked forces through these foundations with the fire of God.

All evil spirits and idolatry shrines ruling there cannot get hold of me. I am not their candidate. Anyone who had included me before my birth in their pagan incantations and spirits' let the fire of God roast and scatter them into desolations; [Psalms 109:1-end],let them die from their roots, in Jesus name, Amen!

With Holy Ghost fire I visit my foundation right from conception and birth, whatever incantations made by anyone over me and my umbilical cords, today I cancel all in Jesus name amen. Any ungodly groups, unholy congregation summoning me in any spiritual court, die and roast by fire of God, in Jesus name Amen. I cancel and come against all concoctions, divinations, enchantments, sorcerers, and bewitchments anyone had done on my behalf or against me; I decree death by strangulation to all who oppose my life and destiny in Jesus name Amen.

By the power that created heaven and earth, I decree I am free from all satanic harassments and assaults, from this day I win, and I experience victory all the way in Jesus name Amen!!!